An Insider's Guide to Commercial Property

BY JOHN HOWARD

ISBN 978-1-3999-9543-6

CONTENTS

ABOUT THE AUTHOR

John Howard is one of the UK's most experienced property consultants, developers, traders, and investors, with over four decades of experience within the industry. John's extensive expertise stems from the sale and purchase of over 4,000 houses, apartments, and developments across the UK: from traditional houses to hotels and large scheme developments. One of John's more recent projects being the £27 million construction of 150 apartments at Ipswich Waterfront.

Today, John shares the knowledge accumulated during his career through his books, seminars, and mentoring, helping others navigate the complexities of property investment and development.

ACKNOWLEDGEMENTS

Thank you to Ruby Howard for her assistance in editing this book; your contributions have been instrumental in shaping this work. I also extend my thanks to Tiffany Howard for her efforts on our current and future commercial property projects.

I would like to express my appreciation to the commercial agents I've had the pleasure of working with, and those I look forward to collaborating with in the future. Your partnership has been, and will remain, essential to my journey.

CHAPTER 1
RENTAL YIELDS

For many years now, investing in commercial property has been a successful move for me. Leases tend to be longer than for residential properties, you are typically renting a space for five years or longer; giving you a steady income stream for years to come. Your tenant is also likely to be in the property during the day throughout the week, minimising the risk of late-night and weekend maintenance issues, unlike in my residential portfolio.

Commercial property is valued based on yield if tenanted, and estimated yield if it is vacant.

WHAT IS A RENTAL YIELD?

Rental yield indicates what we can expect as a return on investment from rent received. It is a percentage figure that reflects annual rental income compared to the value of the property.

Rental yield is calculable by dividing the annual income of the property, by the value and then multiplying this figure by 100. For example, if you purchased a property for £100,000 and a tenant is giving you £10,000 per annum in rent, the rental yield would be 10%.

£10,000 divided by £100,000 x 100 = 10%.

Knowing the rental yield of a property is very important before you part with your hard-earned money. You need to ensure that you will be receiving enough income to make a profit. Crucially, any lender will also want to know that you are able to pay back the loan. It's most likely they will want to know the net yield, but the gross yield can be a handy figure to know.

The gross yield is the total income you will receive, and net yield is the money you can expect to receive after paying any associated costs, such as maintenance and insurance. In the case of a full repairing and insuring lease, which I will discuss later, your net and gross yield will be the same.

STRENGTH OF COVENANT

This terms refers to the ability of the tenant to pay their rent. The word covenant is somewhat archaic and essential means a formal agreement between two or more parties, in this case, between a landlord and tenant.

Take a lock-up shop, for example, that is going to be let to a local company new to business. They have no personal guarantee, which means there is no legal commitment from a third party to pay the rent should the leaseholder be unable to do so. Assuming the lease is for five years or less, this would be one of the weakest covenants you could have. I would suggest it is worth a yield of approximately 12% for this particular example. If we assume the rent is £7,000 per annum, to calculate rental yield:

1. Take your property's annual rental income

2. Take your property's purchase price, or current market value

3. Divide the annual rental income by the purchase price/ market value

4. Multiply the result by 100 to give you the percentage yield

To work out the value of the lock-up shop above based on a 12% yield you do the following:

1. Take the property's annual rental income (£7,000)

2. Multiply the annual income by 100 - £7,000 x 100 = £700,000

3. Divide this figure by the yield - £700,000 ÷ 12 (the yield) = £58,333

The property value on a 12% yield would therefore be approximately £58,333.

If we consider the example of Barclays Bank. They have a 25-year lease on the premises, paying rent of £50,000 per annum, with at least ten years remaining on the lease. With this example, I would be confident of a rental yield of approximately 5%, which makes the property worth in the region of £1 million.

These are two very simple examples of calculating yield and property value. There are other factors which need to be taken into consideration when calculating both yield and value, which we will discuss going forward.

<u>LENGTH OF LEASE</u>

It's not difficult to understand that a longer lease on a property provides the landlord with a greater sense of security. It makes it less likely that a property will soon become vacant, and leave you with the challenge of finding a new tenant.

When I first began investing in commercial property, it was not uncommon for a tenant to sign a 21- or 25-year lease, with rent reviews every three years that were upward only. However, things have changed dramatically in recent years.

There is now less demand for certain types of commercial property, primarily shops and offices in town centres. In most cases, tenants are unwilling to take a lease for more than three to five years. If you are fortunate enough to secure a tenant who is prepared to take a longer lease, they may insist on a break clause, allowing them to terminate the lease at certain points along the tenancy timeline. In my opinion, a long lease with break clauses still functions as though it were a short lease from the landlord's perspective, as they are still able to vacate the premises without a penalty. By this, I mean a nine-year lease with a break clause after three years, in my view, serves as a three-year lease.

You should be aware of a little-known fact about break clauses: if a tenant is in arrears at the time of the break clause, most leases will not allow them to exercise their rights to break the lease. So, if a break clause is coming up, I recommend perhaps relaxing a little when it comes to chasing them for the rent. If the tenant wishes to implement the break clause and they cannot afford to pay you the arrears, you might be able to legally refuse the notice they must serve to break the lease. However, you should seek legal advice from your solicitor on this matter.

As always, there are exceptions to the rule. Logistic companies that supply organisations like Amazon are prepared to take long leases, as are most supermarket distribution centres. I discuss this in greater detail later in this book.

For now, you can appreciate the importance of the length of lease to an investment. Even if you are in the situation where a tenant like Barclays Bank is paying a high rent but they only have two or three years remaining on the lease and don't intend to renew, you could be left with a property that is vacant and worth half of what it would be otherwise. This is a situation that is happening right now, up and down the country. Where landlords were once receiving £100,000 per annum from an investment, they may now be receiving only £50,000 per annum, and that is assuming the landlord can even find a suitable tenant. In the meantime, a landlord is left paying the empty rates. Even when landlords have a tenant that wishes to remain, tenants are negotiating down the terms, knowing the position that landlords are in.

An example of this is a purchase I made in Ipswich. It was a property with the majority let to BrightHouse, a company with stores across the UK selling white goods. BrightHouse was paying an annual rent of £165,000 with only one year remaining on the current lease. I estimated that if I were able to get them to renew their lease, this would likely be in the region of £50,000 to £60,000 per annum.

I managed to negotiate them to renew at £65,000 per annum, including a further four shops and 15,000 ft^2 of first and second floor space, for which I had obtained permitted development rights for conversion to 30 flats. I paid £900,000 for the building and within four months sold it on for £1.6 million.

Unfortunately for the buyer, BrightHouse shortly afterwards went into administration, leaving them with 8,000 ft^2 of vacant store and liable for the empty rates.

The first two questions I always ask the selling agent are what the current rate per annum is, and how long the lease is and if it includes break clauses. It's vital to know the length of the lease to assess the stability of rental income. And finally, if there are any personal guarantees to support rent payments.

CHAPTER 2
PERSONAL GUARANTEES

A personal guarantee from a tenant is one of the first things I look for in a lease. If the lease is in the name of a person, then you automatically have one. However, if the lease is in the name of their company, then it is essential that you have some guarantee that the rent will be paid. The possibility of personal bankruptcy, even if they have to sell their own home, is the most effective way to focus a tenant's mind!

Today, I find that I encounter all sorts of compromises that don't entail a full personal guarantee. One example is limiting the guarantee to two years of the rent, rather than having a full and unlimited guarantee.

I have a commercial premises which is used as a haulage yard, where a personal guarantee could not be obtained. In this case a rent deposit was agreed. This requires the tenant to give the landlord a sum of money to hold, in the event that the rent is not paid. The difficulty here is that once the rent deposit has run out, and we assume the tenant is not in a position to pay the rent, they are then completely off the hook and able to walk away from the lease. This leaves you with the challenge of finding a new tenant and paying the empty rates on the property until you do.

If the tenant is what is referred to as a national covenant, for example, a large supermarket chain or a commercial enterprise with numerous outlets across the UK, it is highly unlikely that they will offer a personal guarantee from any of their directors. They will instead ask that you rely on the strength of the company that is signing the lease, which may be perfectly acceptable if their accounts are able to demonstrate that they are a cash-rich and successful company. However, even then, the company be taken over, asset stripped, and weakened, as in the example of BrightHouse.

Ultimately, unless the lease is in the name of an individual person, it is essential that you have either a guarantee or a large rent deposit. If the lease is in the name of a company with several directors, then there should be a personal guarantee from all the directors. It is worth noting here that a joint and several guarantee is far better than individual guarantees. The reason for this is that with the former, you are able to seek out the one guarantor with the most assets and get the full amount of the guarantee from them. It is then up to that individual to get their share of the monies back off the other guarantors. In the case of an individual guarantee you are responsible for getting a share of the money from each person.

Whilst we are on the topic of guarantees, during my time as a director of Cambridge United, the club was in the Championship. In 1992, when going for the play-offs for the Premiership, we had a striker called Dion Dublin. We believed Dion Dublin to be worth in excess of £1 million. Being a small club, we were desperate to hold onto him to see if we could get into the Premiership, especially given we were at the top of the table for a while during the season. Looking back, this was an amazing achievement for such a small club.

However, the bank would not lend us any more money without a joint and several guarantee from all five directors. There was one individual on the board who we knew the bank would go to first, should Dion Dublin not be sold at the end of the season if we didn't get promotion.

I can report that, although we got into the play-offs, sadly we didn't get the promotion. Nonetheless, Dion Dublin was sold for £1 million to Alex Ferguson at Manchester United. Following this, we received a letter from the bank saying our guarantees were no longer required. This was after the one particularly wealthy director told everyone before a game not to mention the guarantee. It turns out his wife was in attendance that day, and she was not aware that it had been signed.

For those of you reading who aren't football fans but might watch 'Homes Under The Hammer', yes, it is the very same Dion Dublin. Not only a great striker, but also a very good presenter.

CHAPTER 3
TYPES OF LEASE

There are several types of commercial lease. These have been listed below, in order of preference from a landlord's perspective.

FULL REPAIRING AND INSURING LEASE (FRI)

The Full Repairing and Insuring lease, often abbreviated to FRI, leaves the tenant responsible for all future repairs and insuring liability. This means that the rent received by the landlord is free of any further costs.

Prior to the tenancy beginning, a Chartered Surveyor will normally undertake a Schedule of Condition Survey. This describes the condition of the building, including photographic evidence. The reasoning is that the property should be handed back to the landlord in the same condition it was received by the tenant at the end of the lease.

A FRI lease includes all the external repairs and decorations, together with any roof repairs, guttering, and so on. Cameras today can issue the date and time when a photograph is taken; such evidence alone can sometimes be used as proof of the condition, rather than going to the cost of a full survey. Depending on a number of factors, you may want a full survey, or you may consider it to be superfluous.

At the end of the lease, there is normally a negotiation that takes place between the landlord and the tenant as to the condition of the property. This is known as dilapidations. A further survey is carried out at the end of the lease to assess the current condition of the building.

The surveyor acting for the landlord will then estimate the cost of the works, if any, to put the property back to the condition it was in when first occupied by the tenant. This is sometimes used as a negotiating point to persuade the tenant to continue occupying the property by renewing the lease because, in certain cases, the cost of putting the property back to good order can run into hundreds of thousands of pounds if it is a large premises. When this happens, there are two usual outcomes: either you, as the landlord, will receive a cheque from the tenant to cover the cost of works, or they will undertake it themselves.

Now, a word of warning to all the budding landlords out there: if you're looking to redevelop the property once vacant possession has been obtained, then, unfortunately, claiming dilapidations has recently been successfully challenged by outgoing tenants. The argument is that if you were going to remodel the property for another purpose, therefore the works needed to be completed by the tenant would be deemed unnecessary.

I know of a firm of solicitors who, after many years, were unable to terminate the lease of their offices at the end of the lease term due to the poor condition it was in. It would have cost over £1 million to put it back to the condition which it was originally let to them, and they did not have the money to pay the landlord or to carry out the works required. Therefore, they had to continue renting the building, which was double the size they required, until recently. This was because the landlord realised the redevelopment value of the building. I know this because I was interested in buying the property to convert into residential apartments, something that I will talk about later in the book.

I have also recently been on the other side of a dilapidations claim. I own six estate agency offices in Norfolk run under the Fine and Country brand. We lease all the offices. The Norwich branch office came up for lease renewal recently. We were paying rent of £30,000 per annum, and the landlord decided that they wanted to increase the rent to £40,000 per annum on a five-year lease. I offered £20,000 per annum since commercial premises in Norwich city centre, like most, have gone down in rental value. This was refused, so I found alternative premises in a better location for £20,000 per annum on a five-year lease.

I was concerned about the dilapidations as we had spent no money on the office since we moved in, and it was assigned to us from another business. In other words, we took over the lease from another tenant. The landlord's surveyor came round and carried out a Schedule of Condition, comparing it to the original one conducted at the start of the lease. I was fearing the worst; however, they came back to us and said that they thought there was £14,000 worth of work to be completed to bring the property back to the same condition it was in at the start of the lease.

Every tenant has the option to do the work themselves. Often, this can be a much cheaper option. It would not be the first time a landlord has exaggerated the cost of works to return the property to its original condition from a tenant!

However, you could carry out the works yourself and still find that the landlord and his surveyor are not satisfied, these arguments can go on and on, often only being settled in court. Rather than risking any of that hassle, I decided to offer them £10,000 to resolve the matter, and we settled at £12,000.

Ironically, if the landlord had said we could have continued paying the same annual rent of £30,000 I would have done so. This is because of the time and trouble in finding alternative premises, moving, and the associated costs, as well as the dilapidations. However, I am delighted to report that, after nine months and at the time of writing, our previous premises remain vacant. Sometimes, as a landlord, it doesn't pay to be greedy. On a new five-year lease at £40,000 per annum, which I think will be a challenge to achieve, the increase in what we were paying will be eaten up within one year of the property being vacant. A lesson for all of us!

INTERNAL REPAIRING AND INSURING WITH SERVICE CHARGE

The reason you may not be able to have a full repairing and insuring lease (FRI) on a property is that there are other tenants in the building who need to share the costs of any external maintenance. Although not as comprehensive or straightforward as an FRI, this type of lease can be just as effective. However, for it to be so, it will need much more management.

A service charge will have to be calculated, and invoices sent out on a quarterly or a bi-annual basis to prove what costs have been paid to maintain the building. The tenants will then pay their proportion of the costs as per the agreement in the lease, hopefully accumulating 100% of all external costs. Internally, of course, the tenant is responsible for their own maintenance and any repairs, and the insurance would be apportioned within the service charge.

INTERNAL REPAIRING ONLY LEASE

This is one level down from the internal repairing and insuring lease which includes the service charge for the external maintenance. No external expenditure can be recouped from a lease that is only internal repairing. Such leases are normally only granted if the external building is in very poor condition and the tenant is not willing to take on the responsibility and costs associated with repairs. Alternatively, it could be a listed building, which is potentially more costly to repair than a modern building. I talk more about listed buildings in Chapter 14.

LET ON LICENCE

This is a much weaker type of legal letting arrangement and is typically employed when there are numerous tenants in a building, perhaps each renting one room, either as an office or for other commercial activities.

Most let on licences are for a maximum of three years, after which, most solicitors will advise that a comprehensive lease should be signed. As always, please seek advice from your legal representatives in these matters. I'm not a solicitor and would never want to be one!

There are a couple of key differences between a licence and a lease. One is that once the licence period comes to an end, there is no guarantee that the tenant can renew and remain in the premises. The second is that, should the freehold of the property be sold, technically a new licence should be signed with the new owner of the freehold. However, in my experience, this doesn't always happen.

HOLDING OVER

This term is used when the lease or licence has come to an end, but the tenant has remained in the premises, paying rent. If you are looking to purchase a property where this has happened, there is no need to be overly suspicious about this. Quite often, it's because the property is being sold, and the current freeholder does not want to restrict the future owners by renewing a lease.

Your solicitor my express concerns, but in my experience, this situation gives you the opportunity to negotiate a new lease, perhaps with an uplift in the annual rent, or you may even be able to persuade the tenant to reduce the size of their premises. This allows you the possibility to obtain more rent from another party or redevelop the space that the current tenant is vacating.

Over the years, I have purchased many properties where this is the case and I have had minimal issues with any of them in terms of renewing the leases. Of course, there is always the opportunity to renegotiate terms prior to purchasing the property to give you peace of mind.

Should you wish to obtain vacant possession, the more important question to ask is whether the lease adheres to the 1954 Landlord and Tenant Act or whether there is a break clause in the lease that allows you to serve notice to gain vacant possession.

LANDLORD AND TENANT ACT 1954

If a tenant is signed up on a "Protected Lease", this means they have the benefit of security of tenure under the Landlord and Tenant Act 1954. The tenant is entitled to remain in the business premises when the lease expires and, as we discussed above, 'hold over.' The landlord is then obliged to grant the tenant a new lease, generally on similar terms to the one which has just expired.

Quite often there is an option to break the lease under a redevelopment clause.

If the lease is within the Landlord and Tenant Act 1954 and the tenant wishes to renew and serves the notice correctly, you must adhere to that and grant a new lease on similar terms to the one which has just expired.

BREAK CLAUSE

This is a mechanism where one or both parties can break the lease by serving notice on the other at stipulated times, as per the terms of the break clause within the lease. As mentioned earlier, it is quite common for a tenant to have a break clause at three years, and possibly six years, within a nine-year lease. My argument with people who say it's a nine-year lease is that with a break clause at year three, it is only a three-year lease, not a nine–year lease, as it can be surrendered.

A fair compromise is to allow both parties to have a break clause. Should you, as a landlord wish to gain possession at the break for whatever reason, then you can do so; that is providing you have served the correct notice, which I would always instruct a solicitor to do on your behalf.

REDEVELOPMENT BREAK CLAUSE

In certain leases, there may be a clause which allows you to break the lease and obtain vacant possession if you can prove that you are going to redevelop the property. Don't think that, just because the clause is there, you will be successful in obtaining vacant possession without proving, potentially in court, that you have a bona fide development scheme with planning that you can act on once vacant possession is gained.

Back in 1989, I was the proud owner of a parade of shops, above which there was a ballroom dance school run by a very well-known local professional dancer called Olga, who had been in the premises for many years. There was a break clause in the lease for redevelopment, which should have allowed me to obtain vacant possession and redevelop the site. Having obtained planning permission for a restaurant, I visited Olga and explained that I would be serving notice to terminate the lease for redevelopment as per the redevelopment clause in the lease.

I offered Olga 12 months to vacate the premises and find alternative accommodation, thinking that I was doing her a favour. Before I knew it, I was on the front page of the local newspaper, and a campaign was launched to save the dance school. They managed to get 18,000 signatures on a petition!

Needless to say, the local MP also got involved! So, faced with huge opposition to my plans, I decided not to proceed with the redevelopment, and I eventually sold the building to someone much braver than me. After several years, it was finally redeveloped as a restaurant, which I often go to, and I still have the memory of the cartoon that was drawn in the newspaper of myself being shown the door by Olga.

Remember, just because there is a redevelopment break clause in a lease, this doesn't always mean that it works out as you wish!

As a young, ambitious property developer who had been totally humiliated by Olga and the newspaper, I eventually had the pleasure of being able to purchase the newspaper's headquarters and printing works, consequently knocking it down and selling the cleared site on to McCarthy and Stone; a deal, I must say, that I enjoyed more than I should have done!

CHAPTER 4
RENT REVIEWS

Nearly every lease contains a clause for rent reviews. A rent review typically occurs every three to five years; although for larger tenants, this could be every five to seven years. When I am negotiating a new lease with a tenant, I try to negotiate rent reviews as regularly as possible.

Rent reviews used to hold far more importance than they do now, as rents could even double within a term! Today, you are most likely to be grateful that the rent remains the same. As I have already highlighted with my acquisition where BrightHouse was the tenant in Chapter 1, you now know what can and does happen when a lease expires.

Let's now explore what happens at a rent review. The tenant or tenant's surveyor, if they appoint one to act on their behalf to negotiate the rent review, will research the local rental market to collect as much evidence to support their view.

For instance, the shop you own is currently rented at £20,000 per annum and is 1,000 ft^2, the shop next door which is a similar size and condition to yours has had the lease renewed at £10,000 per annum. It is going to be a challenge to secure the same rent as you have previously received when there is evidence to show the shop next door with the same square footage is paying half of that.

I have already demonstrated this to you as a tenant in my Norwich office, where I managed to find a better office for two-thirds of the rent I was previously paying and half the rent that my existing landlord wished to charge on a new lease.

If you are looking to purchase a freehold but there is no clause stating that the rent cannot be reduced, I would be very concerned. I would take advice from a local surveyor who negotiates rent reviews, as they will have all the local evidence to hand and be able to advise you on the likely rental level upon review.

More explicitly, they will advise you what the current zones - A, B, and C - are in the street. Let me explain. With retail premises, professionals work out what the rent should be by dividing the retail space into several zones. Zone A has a depth normally of 6.1 metres from the display window and this is the more valuable space compared to Zones B and C, which are further back. The large commercial agents and surveyors work out all rental values on this basis.

However, when it comes to my assessment of commercial property, I am far more interested in what a tenant is willing and able to pay, rather than the theoretical perspective of a surveyor or agent. Even if you can put the rent up to, say, double what it is currently, is it sensible to do so if the tenant can't afford it?

When negotiating a lease with a new tenant, I always attempt to include upward-only reviews in the lease. Local and regional tenants are most likely to accept such a clause, whereas national ones are less so. If you come across a lease that already has upward-only

RPI-linked or similar rent reviews at specified points, that is very good because there is no additional expense and time taken for negotiation. Again, that is, assuming the tenant can afford to pay the increase.

A few years ago, when I purchased Cambridge United's football stadium from the club. I had been a director there for 15 years, the club found itself in grave financial difficulty. We leased the ground back to them for 50 years and linked the rent reviews to the Retail Price Index (RPI). We did this for two reasons: one - that it stops any negotiating on the rent reviews, and two - that it was very difficult to put a rental value on a football stadium. The initial annual rent was £200,000 after the review, it increased to £235,000 per annum. From this example, you can see that linking the rent review to the RPI is one of the best ways to deal with rent reviews.

Most leases will have one of the following types of review:

- One that can go up or down depending on local rental market and its supporting evidence

- Upward only

- Linked to the retail price index (RPI) or another similar index

- Fixed increases already agreed within the lease

CHAPTER 5
TYPES OF SHOPS

LOCK-UP SHOP

One of the simplest commercial investments, and often a starting place for many commercial investors is a lock-up shop. This is a shop with no additional quarters included. It is either solely the ground floor shop, with the upstairs either retained by the current owner or sold off to another part prior to it being offered for sale.

This type of investment is normally leased to single shop occupiers; tenants with only one retail outlet.

SHOP WITH UPPERS

A shop with uppers is a mixed-use property that has multiple use classes for different floors or areas of the building. A good example would be a ground floor shop with offices on upper levels.

This is a much more flexible investment than a lock-up shop, and one that I have often purchased. The key to these investments is to split any upper floors from the ground floor. In the past, I have obtained planning permission to convert them into flats and then sold these off individually, and more recently, converted them under permitted development rights, which I will discuss later.

In some cases, it may be that the shop and upper floors are let to the same tenant. In this case the upper floors may be undervalued, particularly if they are used as storage by the existing tenant, or even as offices. Negotiating with the existing tenant to relinquish the upper floors can be a great advantage to you, as it gives you the opportunity to redevelop these floors. It's important to remember here that if you plan on doing this, you will need a separate entrance.

When a tenant relinquishes a portion of their lease, this is known as a 'part-surrender of the lease'. This means that a new lease will have to be negotiated, agreed upon and signed with the identified areas. Redeveloping these undervalued spaces will add value to your investment.

LARGER SHOP PREMISES

The premises I am referring to here are normally between 2,000 ft^2 and 10,000 ft^2 on the ground floor. Normally, there is a similar square footage on any upper floors.

Large shop premises currently offer break-up and redevelopment opportunities. However, I am not suggesting that we all go and buy a vacant department store, such as a former Debenhams. These will have very expensive empty rates and overheads. The greatest challenge often posed by very large stores is the size itself. The size and depth are responsible for the lack of windows and natural light. The lack of windows is a challenge when looking to convert the space for alternative use, such as for residential apartments. The depth and the lack of windows can sometimes be dealt with by creating a central core atrium, open to the roof. This allows light into the heart of the building, giving the opportunity to then create apartments or office space. I have often thought twice about taking on buildings like this!

Recently, I made an offer on a vacant Marks & Spencer, these are often slightly smaller than the previous example of a former Debenhams. However, I was gazumped by Mike Ashley for a Sports Direct store. It is a highly unusual to be competing with a potential shop owner on a vacant property. Most retailers do not want to own the freehold, however cheap it may be, much preferring to lease premises as this offers greater flexibility. I am currently negotiating the purchase of another Marks & Spencer, and I hope Mike Ashley will not be interested in this one!

There are currently thousands of vacant shops across the UK, some in fantastic locations. Recently, I had the opportunity to purchase the freehold of a vacant shop in a high street location for £350,000. It is located next door to Marks & Spencer and opposite Next and Primark. Ten years ago, if you had said to me that I would be able to compete in purchasing such a freehold in a high street location, I would have said that you were wrong. The way the market has changed now allows investors like us the opportunity to mix with the big boys!

These types of commercial investments were often previously purchased on low yields by pension funds. They were happy with very low percentage returns on their investments, in some cases as low as 3% or 4%. Most of these buyers have now run for the hills and are no longer interested in buying investments like these! The cause being the demise of the high street and the continual growth of online shopping. The drive up to my house has nearly been worn out, due to vans delivering all sorts of goods daily! Sadly, we are all at fault for allowing our high streets to become what they are today, myself included.

In the property world, a little turbulence and challenging retail trading brings great opportunities for entrepreneurial property investors. So long as we are taking calculated risks, knowing we must pay empty rates while finding a new tenant. The current economic state allows smaller investors the chance to get a look in.

The risk of having one large tenant in a commercial building is that, should the tenant decide to vacate at the end of the lease or if there is a break clause, then you are left with a vacant premises which may be difficult to relet unless you are sensible with your asking rent.

If a property is currently occupied in the town centre, you should assume that upon rent review this is likely to be halved if it is not an upward-only lease. Even in the event that you have an upward-only lease, if the tenant is struggling or cannot pay the current rent, you still have a problem on your hands! Besides, even if the current tenant is trading well, they are likely to try and reduce rent in the current market!

If I had a pound for every time a commercial agent said to me, "Well, it was let for £50,000 per annum and might be slightly less than that now," I would be living in Jersey as a tax exile! Assume it will be half. If it ends up more than half, it will be a nice bonus.

Recently, I turned down the option to purchase such an investment that was let to a very well-known discount shop with two years remaining on their current lease. My reasoning for this was, firstly, they have a very poor reputation within the retail sector and, secondly, I was absolutely convinced that even if the rent was reduced by 50% on renewal, I was not confident that they would remain, having heard a rumour from someone else in the industry that they were looking to reduce all rents by 70%!

It is important to understand the type of tenant that you will be dealing with. In this case, ten years ago, the tenants were running market stalls. Since then, they have taken advantage of the many vacant commercial buildings in town centres. As someone said to me recently, "once a market trader, always a market trader".

PARADE OF SHOPS

A parade of shops is where several shops are situated together. There is often safety in numbers, even if the shops are predominantly on short leases. Even if you lose one or two tenants due to break clauses or end of leases, you are unlikely to lose them all at one time, which should give you confidence in your investment.

As investments, parades of shops are very popular for the reasons already mentioned, so often they sell for a lower yield than an investment with mainly local tenants would. Mainly, these parades are in local shopping areas, not in town centres, and quite often have not been affected so badly by the continued drive towards online shopping.

Investors that tend to buy a parade of shops are quite often local to the investment and subsequently will be more confident about the area and may even know some of the tenants.

Parking is critical to these shops, and the ability to be able to park outside the shops should not be underestimated. Personally, if I were looking to rent a shop outside a town or city centre, I would always want to ensure that it either includes parking or there is a public car park very close by.

CHAPTER 6

SHOP TENANTS AND THE VALUE OF YIELDS

The following is my opinion of the value of different commercial investments. You may consider that I am too tough on some or not harsh enough on others.

The value of a property is dependent on who you ask. If I asked two surveyors to value any given property, then invariably they would come up with two different figures. However, we would expect these to be within a 10% range of each other. As the saying goes, 'You pays your money and you takes your chances.'

BLUE CHIP TENANTS

With the current state of the market, I consider this to be an interesting term for any tenant. For many years, most of the well-known high street brands would have been described as blue chip tenants. Pension funds were clamouring to own such investments on very low yields.

However, with some of our best-known brands now gone, the likes of Woolworths, British Home Stores, Debenhams and many more, once considered to be blue chip tenants are now bankrupt and bust, long gone from our high streets. This begs the question of whether there are many of these blue chip tenants left.

The only ones that are really left now are the supermarkets, charity shops, and new businesses which are now fit for the modern commercial world. However, even when you identify one of these tenants, they are unlikely to be willing to sign long leases, affecting yields and consequently the value of your investments.

I'd like to expand upon my meaning of supermarkets to include local shops in out-of-town locations that are owned by the blue-chip supermarkets, sometimes under a different brand name. Although they are not in prime locations, they remain robust investments.

If you purchase a property with a blue-chip tenant producing a 10% yield, and you believe they will renew their lease, you may have a very good investment on your hand. However, you should be warned that even if they are financially sound, they will also be advised and are likely to try and negotiate their rent down, like many others in the market. Conversely, there are reasons why it's not advantageous for them to reduce their rent as much as possible. For example, if they are trading successfully from their existing premises, it may not be worth the cost and inconvenience to relocate.

Short leases are becoming more and more common, and the investment market must therefore adjust accordingly. I believe that the changes we have witnessed in recent years are here to stay.

Some retailers will want to remain on the high-street, even if it is only to retain a shop window to support their online offering. Furthermore, will a retailer who has been successfully trading, and had a customised shop fitting want to vacate within only a few years?

It's a difficult question to answer, and this is where your intuition and own balanced judgement comes into play.

There are a few basics that need to be covered, such as looking at potential tenants' accounts to understand how strong their online and high-street presence is. It is always worth attempting to establish contact with their estates department to gauge the likelihood of a lease renewal. It may be that they will consider renewing earlier if you enter into negotiations about rent.

As an investment with blue chip tenants, I work to the following rental yields:

- Let on FRI lease with 10 years or more remaining: 6% yield
- Let on FRI lease with 5 years or less remaining: 10% yield (this reflects the potential of a rent reduction or the tenant vacating upon expiry)

NATIONAL TENANTS

National tenants are those with a many national outlets, but are smaller than the blue chip companies, many of which you would find on the FTSE 250. Many national tenants are now looking to reduce their number of outlets, and perhaps are even struggling to remain in business. So, remember this before becoming too impressed with a national tenant that has many locations. Therefore, it is important instead to identify those which are looking to expand. Often, they are ambitious, well-funded, and often willing to pay more than their well-established counterparts. Expanding tenants will pay more to secure a strong position on the high-street.

Once these businesses have expanded into numerous outlets they are often sold. Sometimes as another organisation takes over, they can become over-geared which results in a downhill financial spiral. Of course, sometimes they can benefit from this and grow even greater, but I think it's important to be aware of the risks.

When it comes to national tenants, it is crucial to understand the life cycle of these businesses and where they are amongst this, either as expanding or rescinding outlets. Understanding this progression will allow you to ascertain the strength of the covenant.

When retailers are looking to expand into new locations, they will have their shopping list of requirements. This list then goes to commercial agents across the country, or sometimes to one commercial agent to act on their behalf. If they are looking to cover the entire nation, they normally start with the larger cities in each area, for example, London, Manchester, Birmingham, Leeds, Bristol, Cardiff, Norwich, and others.

For an investment let to a national tenant, I work to the following rental yields:

- Let on FRI lease to an expanding business with ten years or more remaining: 6.5% yield

- Let on FRI lease to a rescinding business with ten years or more remaining: 8% yield

— Let on FRI lease with 5 years or less remaining: 10% yield (this reflects the potential of a rent reduction or the tenant vacating upon expiry).

SECONDARY TOWN CENTRE SHOPS

Secondary town centre shops are defined as those not in the town centre but in a location nearby and often have a wider mix of retail and non-retail uses. I have bought many of these over previous years as investments as they potentially have alternative uses, especially under the new permitted development rights. They tend to be let on shorter leases and, in many cases, to tenants who do not have as strong financial accounts as some of the bigger companies. Often, they are owner-run or smaller companies with two or three branches.

In terms of yield, they are clearly not as strong as the previously mentioned, but many are long-established and successful businesses, which should give you some confidence in the tenant's future ability to pay the rent.

With this type of investment, I work to the following rental yields:

— Let on FRI lease with 5 to 10 years remaining: 8% yield

— Let on FRI lease with 5 years or less remaining: 10% yield

SHOP WITH UPPERS

Shops with uppers are, in my opinion, more difficult to value. The reason for this is that there is sometimes potential in the upper floors which hasn't been effectively utilised and thus isn't reflected in the rent payable. As previously mentioned, a tenant could be using the upper space as storage, and so its value is being reflected in its use as storage space. However, this could be offices, or residential space, adding significant returns on your investment.

I have a personal connection to these types of shops; my father ran a greengrocer out of one many years ago. As did Margaret Thatcher's father, she later described these people as, "the true entrepreneurs" a sentiment I agree with.

These shops are likely to be in residential areas and are sometimes worth more as individual houses, assuming planning can be obtained. However, for this purpose, let us assume that they don't have any unaccounted-for value and that they are leased on internal repairing and insuring leases, with three-year upward only rent reviews.

With this type of investment, I work to the following rental yield:

– Let on IRI lease with 5 years or less remaining: 12% yield

LOCK-UP SHOPS

Lock up shops sit on the lower rungs of the investment ladder for reasons as discussed in the previous chapter. They often attract similar tenants and are in similar locations to shops with uppers.

Lock-up shops tend to attract first-time retailers; those who have always wanted to open their own shop and have now decided to do so. Most of these people want to improve their quality of life and become their own boss. Therefore, most of these tenants are likely to be sole traders, either entirely without financial accounts or relatively weak accounts without an extensive history.

Often, these lock-up shops are let on licence or on a short lease of three years. So, taking the risks into consideration, I would work to the following rental yield:

– Let on an internal repairing only or licence with 3 years remaining: 12% to 15% yield

CHAPTER 7
OFFICES

One of the many types of commercial property that you may choose to invest in is offices. Often when people are considering their venture in the world of commercial property, the mind immediately jumps to shops. Similarly to shops, offices come in all shapes and sizes; from larger blocks to small individual units. Additionally, in recent years, we have seen an explosion in the number of serviced offices and co-working spaces.

At the time of writing, in the UK, there is currently vacant office space that is equivalent to fifty times the square footage of the O2 in London. Experts suggest that around 50% of current office space could still yet be reduced.

We have all felt significant changes in our day-to-day lives since the COVID 19 pandemic. The world stood still for a short while, and then when it all started back up, we had jumped a decade forward. Whilst I feel that the 50% figure previously mentioned is somewhat exaggerated, I do think a 25% reduction would be quite realistic.

I appreciate that working for home is ideal for many and can benefit the quality of life for individuals and their families, it also presents its own unique challenges. Working entirely from home can make managing your work and home life balance very difficult. I think some people, either at their own request or at the request of their employer, will return to the office full time, and some will adopt a hybrid work routine.

Following the COVID-19 pandemic, we saw a shift in the market and an influx of large purpose-built offices varying from 10,000 ft^2 to 100,000 ft^2. It's my opinion going forward that fewer and fewer will be occupied by single tenants, with many being let on a floor-by-floor basis. Although there is still some demand from large multinationals and government departments, and these tenants are often prepared to sign leases of 15 or more years.

However, this trend started well before 2020, over the last 30 years, there has been a gentle stream of vacant offices coming on the market. This has provided opportunities to developers, like myself, who have converted these into residential spaces. However, today we see an avalanche of large office blocks becoming available, which would be in desperate need of refurbishment prior to being relet as offices. Most are far more profitable when converted to residential, rather than to refurbish and let to commercial tenants.

LARGER MODERN OFFICES

If you are looking to purchase one of these types of investments, I would be very careful of asbestos; it's found in many premises constructed during the 1960s, 1970s, and early 1980s. An essential part of your due diligence should be an asbestos report.

Moreover, the tenants of today expect air-conditioning alongside other modern facilities. If the office is currently occupied by one tenant, this could be a dangerous game to play, unless they are considered a blue chip tenant with many years remaining on the lease.

Owing to their size, many of these offices are let to different companies, commonly referred to as multi-let investments. It will be to the detriment of the rental yield, but personally, I am happy with that as it makes the investment safer. You do not have all your 'eggs in one basket!'

MEDIUM SIZE MODERN OFFICES (5000 FT² TO 10,000 FT²)

For many investors, these are a more manageable-sized building. If a tenant does vacate, there are potentially alternative uses, including redevelopment, which is fundable for most investors.

As investments, these are attractive to those with cash funds in their pensions. Pension funds can often be used to purchase commercial property. Some buy them as investments, others self-occupy and rent the building back to their own company.

If you are bidding against someone who is buying the building for themselves, the likelihood is that you will be outbid by them, and in honesty, that is exactly how it should be. I am always suspicious if I am the highest bidder, especially when purchasing one of these popular-sized office investments.

SMALL MODERN OFFICES (UP TO 5,000FT^2)

These are very similar to medium-sized office buildings, but even more popular with owner-occupiers. I have not mentioned parking yet, which, of course, is highly desirable, even if it is only for the managing director and the chairman.

Being out of town is also advantageous, particularly for access and parking. In my experience, most employees like to be based in a town centre, enabling them to go shopping or for lunch during their break. On balance, ease of access and avoiding daily traffic congestion, alongside the cost of all-day parking in out-of-town locations, beats any potential downside in my opinion.

OLDER CONVERTED OFFICES

Many buildings, originally built as houses, especially in town and city centres, have now been converted to offices. Traditionally, solicitors have found this type of accommodation very attractive to occupy. The downside is that many come with little or no parking. I speak from experience; as a client, visiting my solicitor and not having any where to park is very inconvenient.

If you are buying such a building as an investment, you must always have one eye on the alternative use for the building should the tenant vacate or not renew at the end of their lease. Also, depending on the current condition of the building, it can be challenging to secure a new tenant on a fully repairing and insuring lease.

I am currently purchasing such a building in a market town to convert into residential accommodation. The current state of the building is very poor; I am surprised that anybody would want to work in the building in its current condition, but this isn't uncommon. I have viewed a number of older converted offices over the years to revert back to residential, and in many cases, they are vacant as the tenant is moving to more modern premises in a similar location.

SERVICED OFFICE ACCOMMODATION

This is a rapidly expanding investment area. There are large national and international serviced office companies which specialise in this. Often, these specialist companies lease the entire office block themselves and then sublet on a room-by-room basis.

I am sure most of you are aware that you can rent one room in a large block, have the office phone answered on your behalf in the name of your company, share a boardroom, and so on. For many, this is a very convenient way of working. I am always surprised how affordable this type of accommodation can be, even in cities like London.

When I go to Canary Wharf to film for Property TV, their studio is located within a larger office building. On the ground floor, there are currently putting in a coffee area and gym, which I do find slightly surprising as there is a Pret A Manger next door!

In London and other major cities, this is increasingly common with many serviced office companies doing the same.

However, I'm not suggesting that we should go and buy large serviced accommodation blocks in central London, but you may be interested in more modest buildings to use for the same purpose. When looking at occupancy, I would be cautious how often you have 100% occupancy. I would calculate your figures at 70% occupancy in a strong market and 50% in a depressed market.

Remember, you will be paying the overheads such as the rates, unless you can get every room rated individually by the council. You will also be responsible for paying for the electricity and heating costs as well as all repairs. Serviced accommodation investments do require intensive management.

If you are looking to the future, then this is perhaps an investment to investigate further. I believe serviced office accommodation will continue to grow in popularity, especially if it benefits from parking. Particularly as the desire to work in large cities every day is diminishing.

Business hubs which offer flexible working alongside networking opportunities provide a great alternative to those who do not wish to work from home all of the time but, do not want or cannot afford to lease large office spaces.

VALUE / RENTAL YIELD OF OFFICES

With office investments I work to the following rental yields:

- A modern office building over 10,000 ft^2 with a FRI lease, let to a blue chip covenant with 10 years remaining: 5% yield

- A modern office building over 10,000ft^2 with a FRI lease, let to a national covenant with 10 years remaining: 6.5% yield

- A modern office building 5,000ft^2 or less with a FRI lease, let to a local covenant with 5 to 10 years remaining: 8% yield

- A older office building 5,000ft^2 or less with a FRI lease, let to a local covenant with 5 to 10 years remaining: 9% yield

Remember, this is my opinion, others may differ, but we should be within a 10% valuation of one other.

CHAPTER 8
WAREHOUSING AND DISTRIBUTION CENTRES

For many years, warehouses have been considered a very basic investment, and generally were not particularly popular. In the trade, these are often described as 'sheds': relatively easy to obtain planning and cost effective to build – but, were never easy to let and certainly not on a long lease.

However, times are changing! Where other types of commercial property, for example, shops on the high street, are suffering, warehouses are benefitting from online retailing coming to the fore.

Today, warehousing and distribution centres are often the 'hottest ticket' in town. Previously, rental yields could be anywhere between 10% and 15%. Now, with a strong covenant and long lease, a 4% yield is acceptable: a remarkable turnaround. Pension funds, which previously would have invested in the high street and now turning to warehousing as a 'safe' investment for their clients.

Looking at the success of companies, like Amazon, which need distribution centres across the UK, it was always going to happen.

Now for some facts. In the UK, there are currently 566,000,000 ft^2 of warehousing and it is worth approximately £127 billion to the economy. According to experts, we will run out of warehouse space within 12 months.

When we refer to 'warehouse space', we are referring to the very large distribution centres, which are currently springing up on the sides of motorways up and down the country. To invest in these distribution centres requires serious financial clout.

There is also an increase in smaller units, some new and some which have been converted from farm buildings and the like. I would consider these to be a safe investment in the future, and with a warehousing shortage on the horizon, I believe you can expect the annual income for one of these to increase.

Recently, I was speaking to a commercial agent who is currently negotiating a rent review on behalf of a client renting a small warehousing unit. Their rent is increasing from £5 /ft^2 to £11 /ft^2. There was little the agent could do for his client to reduce this further, as this is in line with the local market prices.

If any of you have recently purchased a small industrial estate, which includes a warehousing distribution centre of any size, you should feel very satisfied with your investment.

Many small estates were created in the 1980s when government grants and tax rebates were available to investors, with the purpose of stimulating the local economy. These were often called 'starter units' and are still popular today with businesses from printing to tyre companies and everything in between.

One consideration to have if you are considering the purchase of a small industrial estate is that the roads are often not adopted, and as such need maintaining at the expense of the freeholder. Although, you may be able to claw back these costs via service charges, but you should check the leases to see if you are able to do so.

Usually, the smaller industrial estates are made up of a number of small units with individual leaseholders. If your estate is made up of say, ten individual units, you would be incredibly fortunate to have all of the tenants pay on time and have all units simultaneously occupied. This is true even in the strong market today. Small businesses that occupy these types of units can fail, even in a strong economy.

As I mentioned previously, some units have been converted from farm buildings, heavy industry and more. This brings me to another opportunity: converting these existing buildings. One thing I stress here is the importance of location. You really need proximity to the main road network; if not, this will affect your rental value and yields.

You can also maximise your potential yield if a building has good ceiling height, by taking the opportunity to install a mezzanine floor. In a warehouse, the mezzanine becomes the first-floor accommodation. Most of the time, the £/ft^2 is less than the ground floor, but it is still well worth investing in.

There is also always the opportunity to refurbish existing stock, particularly those built some years earlier. Refurbishment of warehousing mainly consists of renewing the external cladding, which will give them a more modern and vibrant feel.

With warehouse investments, I work to the following rental yields:

- A new warehouse on a large distribution centre let to a blue chip covenant, FRI with 10 years remaining: 4.5% yield

- A modern warehouse on a small distribution centre let to a national covenant, FRI with 10 years remaining: 6% yield

- A refurbished warehouse less than 5,000 ft^2 centre let to a local covenant, FRI with 5 to 10 years remaining: 7% yield (these are very popular with local investors)

RETAIL WAREHOUSES

Retail warehouses came to the fore as investments in the 1980's at a similar time that supermarkets began moving to out-of-town locations. Most local authorities allowed planning permission for large out-of-town retail parks which would previously have been opposed. The popularity of these has continued to increase, often because there is an abundance of parking right outside.

Councils have now realised that these out-of-town shopping centres have had a detrimental effect on the high streets, and many are now trying to stop any more from popping up. Sadly, the phrase 'closing the stable door after the horse has bolted' comes to mind. I think it's safe to say that the councils are a little too late on this.

Many commercial developers who have identified land, have profited from obtaining planning permission and building these out-of-town retail parks; some retaining their investments and others selling to pension funds and investors.

Today, when granting planning permission for these out-of-town centres, councils often impose conditions that require large companies to also have a high street presence. I do wonder what happens in the event that these companies wish to close their town centre store when they find it is losing money. With the grant of planning permission, it is likely that a Section 106 agreement will need to be signed.

A Section 106 agreement is an agreement between a developer and a local planning authority about measures that the developer must take to reduce their impact on the community. In this example, the s106 would prohibit the retailer from closing the town centre shop. With a good planning consultant, I am sure it will be possible to argue the closure if it was unprofitable to remain open. I mention this because some investors may be tempted to purchase one of these town centre retail outlets leased by a big retailer. Be aware that they may try to close it in the future.

Many retail warehouses are operated by large national and international companies; fewer are owned by small private companies. In terms of investments, due to their size and rental value, many are being purchased by pension funds and large investment companies.

If you have the opportunity and are brave enough, purchasing a vacant unit that can then be split into smaller units is an investment I would seriously consider. We will discuss vacant units in more detail in chapter 12.

With retail warehouse investments, I work to the following rental yields:

– Let on FRI to a blue chip covenant with 10 years
  remaining: 6% yield

- Let on FRI to a national covenant with 10 years remaining: 7% yield

- Let on FRI to a local covenant with 5 to 10 years remaining: 8.5% yield

CHAPTER 9
ALTERNATIVE INVESTMENT PROPERTIES

Having discussed the most popular - shops, offices, and warehouses – let us now discuss alternative commercial investments. For the smaller investor with a good appetite for risk, these can be of interest. Throughout my career, I have invested in many discussed in this chapter.

For those in industries that find it more difficult to secure a premises, perhaps because they create noise or pollution, they will need to pay more rent per square foot than is the local market average. These constraints on where they can operate from allow landlords to command a higher price.

I am a director of a company that owns a commercial yard with offices. A local haulage company approached us when their current premises lease was expiring. They require an operator's licence; they have a fleet of HGV's which move goods. The licence is issued by the Traffic Commissioner – the independent regulator of the commercial road transport industry. It is a lengthy process, and they can be difficult to obtain, fortunately they were successful in obtaining one. The haulage company was well established and wanted to continue trading but was very limited in the sites they could operate from; we therefore receive a premium in rent for this site.

With some alternative commercial investments, the rent is not always the most important factor to the tenant. Commercial surveyors who value these premises are often baffled when a tenant is willing to pay considerably more than what they consider the market value. Ultimately, if a business is making very good profit, sometimes there are other considerations that are unique to a particular tenant and make your property more appealing than an alternative.

Generally, these tenants are less likely to vacate or try to reduce the rent upon expiration of their lease. Often because replacing their current premises is difficult and time consuming. As the saying goes, 'if it ain't broke, don't fix it!'

The following is only a personal guide to what an investor might pay for alternative commercial investments. You may decide to pay more or less than I would, hopefully no more than 10% either side of those indicated below.

RESTAURANTS

I have owned numerous investments that have been run as restaurant, and they still interest me. A key point to remember is that up to 50% of restaurants fail in the first year.

Most restaurants are fitted out to a good standard; this is normally the responsibility of the tenant. At the point of writing, I am currently negotiating the rent for a new Chinese restaurant to go in a building which is currently just a shell finish. It does have windows and glass installed, but internally it is bare. Many commercial developers do not put the windows or glass in, instead they are left boarded up; I am sure you have seen many like this. The reason being is, the windows are often broken, and it is difficult to get insurance on vacant buildings. My potential tenant is very keen to take the unit but requires help with the initial rent and the cost of fitting the restaurant out. So, you must decide whether you need to begin looking for another tenant, or if you can make the deal work; perhaps you do some of the fit-out work yourself or negotiate a longer-rent free period. Ultimately, you want to come to an agreement that works for everyone involved.

In recent years, many national restaurant chains expanded across the UK, paying premium rents and spending hundreds of thousands of pounds on fitting these out. Sadly, many are now in administration or have gone bankrupt, thus leaving landlords with an empty, well fitted-out restaurant. In my experience, there is always someone who is willing to take on a restaurant, especially if it has been fitted out to a high standard. I would point out commercial kitchens are very expensive to fit, and in some cases, will have been removed and sold by the previous tenant to claw back some of the original costs.

With restaurants, I work to the following rental yields:

- Let on FRI lease to a national covenant with 10 years remaining: 7% yield

- Let on FRI lease to a local covenant with 5 to 10 years remaining: 9% yield

TAKEAWAY BUSINESSES

A take-away only restaurant often operates in very modest areas and generally poor conditions. There is real value in the fact that such premises have obtained planning permission from the local authority for take-away food; this is often difficult to obtain.

As is the case with restaurants, and perhaps even more so with takeaway businesses, there is always someone willing to have a go and run one. They can be very lucrative, and the tenants are often willing to pay more rent than a commercial surveyor thinks the premises are worth, this is because obtaining planning permission for a takeaway licence can be very difficult; while the surveyor may consider it over-rented someone else may think the price is appropriate for what can be a very profitable business. I have been the proud owner of a kebab shop in Ipswich for well over 30 years and had never had a vacant month during that time, which is testament really to the robustness of takeaway investments.

– Let to a local covenant, rack rented, FRI lease 5 to 10 years: 11% yield

BETTING SHOPS

In the 1980s and 1990s, there was a massive increase in the number of betting shops across the UK, most of them owned by national and international businesses. In the past, they have made excellent investments. You could argue that some are blue chip tenants and even though the properties are not normally in prime locations but in secondary areas of towns and cities, this doesn't detract from the fact that the majority are let to incredibly successful companies with amazingly strong balance sheets.

Rarely do you hear of a bookmaker ever going bankrupt. Unfortunately for the landlords, in recent years, with the increase in online gambling, many of these companies no longer see these shops as beneficial to their operation and are reducing their property estate.

I recently purchased a parade of shops with flats above in Buxton, Derbyshire, a very nice spa town. One of the shops was let to William Hill bookmakers. They had quite recently refurbished the shop, which suggested that they were likely to remain at the end of their lease, which had two years to run. I was very tempted to keep it as they were such a good covenant; however, slightly regretfully, I decided to put it in an auction and sell. It went for an 8.5% yield which, at the time, I felt was probably decent but still held on to the idea that perhaps I should have kept it. That was until a few months ago when, driving past the shop, I noticed it was closed and available to rent. That's one decision I got right!

– Let to a national covenant, FRI lease over 10 years: 6.5% yield

– Let to a local covenant, FRI lease 5 to 10 years: 8.5%

CHARITY SHOPS

I've included charity shops in this chapter because although they are retail, they are such an important part of any high street these days. How many times have you heard over the last few years from shoppers that the "high streets are just full of charity shops and coffee shops"? My response is "thank goodness they are", as what would the high street look like without them!

The reason there are so many charity shops is that even I could make money out of a retail shop if I pay virtually no rates. Most councils only charge charity shops 20% of the overall rate bill and have volunteers running most of the shops, with the only paid employee being the manager. On top of that, all the stock has been given to them. Most landlords are incredibly grateful to these charities for taking up the vacant spaces. Can you imagine how much extra retail space there would be empty if it wasn't for them!

Many of these charities are very big organisations and come under the national covenant title, if not, in certain cases, blue chip if the leases are long enough. You very rarely ever hear of a charity getting into financial difficulty unless they are just a locally run one.

A few years ago, I let a shop to a local Christian charity run by a rather odd leader who also ran a church where the worshippers had to give 10% of their wages to the organisation every month. When I heard this, I was delighted to rent to them as safety in numbers, I thought. The leader also asked me if I'd like to join the church. Now, one rule I do have is that I don't get involved, financially or in any other way, with my commercial tenants, apart from asking them for the rent!

About a year later, the monthly rent started being late and eventually didn't appear at all. I went to see the church leader who asked if he could "share a problem with me". I stupidly said he could and of course, the problem was that they could not pay the rent. There's one good thing about letting to Christians though, as, although I allowed them to vacate the premises, they agreed to rent payments and I was paid every month until the arrears were all paid. While they were in occupation, they very kindly refurbished the whole building for me including the central heating, so I let them off the interest!

- Let to a national charity, FRI lease 10 years: 7%

- Let to a local charity, FRI lease 5 to 10 years: 9%

PUBS

Some of you might be surprised that I've included pubs, but these days not all pubs are owned by the breweries, some have been sold off by them and become owner-occupied and others have eventually ended up for rent. There are 7,600 pubs operating in the UK today, which is a decrease of 13,600 since the year 2000 and I would suggest many of the ones still running make very modest profits.

In the 1990s, a number of sharp-witted property investors realised that some of these pub companies were seriously undervalued in terms of their property portfolios. Now, as it happens, they were right, but the only slight problem with pubs is that most must remain as such, even though there are too many in the country and people's habits have changed.

I find these pubs as commercial buildings incredibly hard to value, partly because the upper floors are normally occupied for residential purposes, and it all depends on the trade being carried out downstairs. One of the challenges is putting a market rent on them because of the situation with the rates that are payable to the local authorities.

In their wisdom, the council works out the rates pub landlords should pay based on their turnover. Now, in principle, that might sound quite a sensible idea, but the problem is that if you get a great tenant who makes a great success of the business and has a high turnover and subsequently decides to sell to another party, suddenly that turnover can reduce dramatically, and the new tenant will still be paying the same rates as the last one. All of which means you could have had a tenant who could pay quite handsomely to be in occupation, and then a different tenant comes along and can no longer pay the rent.

The breweries also have a very big say in what goes on as unless the tenant has a free house (in other words, they can buy their beers from anywhere they wish) they are tied to a brewery and, as such, they pay whatever the brewery demands rent wise, depending on how many barrels of beer they sell. I do appreciate that a lot of pubs these days sell food as much as they do alcohol; however, I'm sure you understand the challenges that they face.

With many existing premises still owned by the breweries and with tenants paying exorbitant rents, it's very easy to start to think that these high rents are attainable when you're looking for a tenant for your recently purchased pub. However, the fact that the brewery sold it at some point, presumably because they struggled to find a tenant to run it anymore, should ring alarm bells.

I have a great friend who owns 150 freehold pubs and has most of them rented out. At one time, he was able to force the tenants to purchase their beer from a certain brewer who then paid my friend, the landlord, commission on the amount of beer the pub sold, which was a great idea while it lasted. The problem was that the tenants couldn't make enough money, and many of the pubs became vacant.

Many pubs were originally houses, and I expect some of you are thinking that it wouldn't be such a bad thing if they were converted back into residential. No doubt you would also like to build on the car park! Over the years, I purchased several vacant pubs in order to convert them into residential, and this is something I cover later on in the book. But please don't think that it is easy or always a viable alternative, because sometimes it's not.

- Let to a national chain, FRI 10 years: 7%

- Let to a local tenant, FRI 5 to 10 years: 11%

LEISURE

A strange title, you might think, for a group that encompasses nightclubs, casinos, bowling, snooker clubs, and any other leisure and late-night entertainment venues. The first thing I would say is, if you speak to banks about acquiring a leisure investment, many will run a mile! The others will just try and charge you a higher interest rate.

The reason for this is they are perceived to be riskier investments and, as we all know, banks are risk averse.

When I was in my 20s and 30s, my dream was to buy a nightclub investment, but probably for the wrong reasons. I did manage to buy a wine bar, as they were called in those days, and that was the next best thing back then.

The reason that banks dislike this type of investment is that, historically, many of these types of businesses had a history of going bankrupt and are perceived to be run by people who may have had a chequered past. Certainly, these days, I don't think that this is the case, and there are large organisations that run these types of entertainment venues across the UK. Not only that, but they spend huge amounts of money fitting out such establishments. As with other alternative investments, there is always someone who will take over a vacant nightclub, for instance, and get it back up on its feet.

In terms of valuing an investment like this, it can be quite difficult because there could be an inflated rent since they require large spaces in secondary areas which, in reality, would not normally rent out for very much. However, because of the planning they have, which will include a late-night licence which is not easy to obtain, quite often tenants of this type will pay an inflated rent.

– Let to a national covenant, FRI 10 years: 9%

– Let to a local tenant, FRI 5 to 10 years: 13%

COFFEE SHOPS

I am personally delighted with everyone's current obsession with coffee. The good thing about coffee is that there is a very big markup.

As I write, I have an empty shop in Colchester for which I have a potential tenant who wishes to open a coffee shop. As if there are not enough already in Colchester, but there we go, I'm overjoyed.

Not many of us can hope to have a Costa or a Starbucks as tenants. They both spend large sums on fitting out their premises and will take long leases. However, I do know of a Starbucks that was let for £105,000 per annum. Then, they decided that the rent was far too high and the building has been vacant for the last two years, which goes to show that even the biggest companies in the business have a limit to what they are willing to pay.

What has helped many of these coffee shops is that the planning rules have softened and changed and now allow the sale of takeaway drinks, as well as the sale of drinks consumed on the premises, together with hot food. Until recently, the planning laws would not allow food to be cooked on the premises. However, this has now changed, and coffee shops no longer have an excuse for the warmed up, pre-packaged food we all consume in them.

When talking about Costa and Starbucks, I'm specifically talking about their town-centre premises. The out-of-town, drive-through, purpose-built units are a very different market. I cover developing this type of unit for specific tenants later.

– Let to a national covenant, FRI 10 years: 6% yield

— Let to a local covenant, FRI 5 to 10 years: 9% yield

CARE HOMES

I have included care homes as, in the current climate, many of them are for sale. Many will have been converted from existing houses, and in many cases will have been extended, sometimes by purchasing the neighbouring property and joining them up. Whatever the case, many of these care homes have been very profitable in the past, and not surprisingly so when you consider that they are comparable to a three-star hotel that has 100% occupancy, whereas most hotels run at about 60% to 65% occupancy at best, and you don't need a chef.

A few years ago, I had the opportunity to purchase a small portfolio of care homes from the existing owners who wanted to lease them back from me. At the time, I was concerned that the yield of 8% was not enough, considering the number of properties that were in poor condition and yet, they were going to rent them anyway without improving them.

Since then, many of the regulations surrounding care homes have changed, and some of these new regulations are not possible to implement in converted homes. Therefore, these have come on the market for alternative uses. I recently purchased one to convert back to houses.

There are some very big players in the purpose-built care home sector. They will pay over £1 million per acre for land subject to planning permission in good residential locations. Many of these companies work alongside an investment company that purchases and develops the sites for them, in return for a long-term lease signed by the care home company.

- Purpose-built let to a national covenant, FRI 10 years: 6.5% yield

- Converted let to a local covenant, FRI 5 to 10 years: 9%

STUDENT ACCOMMODATION

Student accommodation is ultimately a commercial investment, not a residential one. There are 681,000 student rooms across the UK, and in 2020/21 alone, an extra 24,799 rooms were developed. Virtually all this new accommodation has been created by large developers that are building out new student blocks across the UK. It's a very lucrative business, and thus, pension funds are also involved in this type of investment.

The issue for investors is that, in the old days, the university itself would sign up to the leases to then sublet to their students, but nowadays they will no longer do that, and you are dealing directly with students. Competition for letting these rooms has increased greatly, with many universities themselves developing new accommodation on campus. The question I would be asking myself is, "Are the rooms going to rent well if there is competition more convenient to, or on, the campus?"

As a landlord, you really have two choices: do you want to deal directly with the students and have periods with empty accommodation, which will make a large dent in the return on your investment, or let the whole building to a specialist company who will manage the block and let out the rooms directly to the students? You will receive less rent that way but hopefully it will be guaranteed, if the company leasing from you is financially strong enough and the lease is long enough that it will still be worth a decent investment yield.

Most students will probably rent these rooms for a maximum of 42 weeks of the year. Some people will tell you that you can rent the other weeks out to international students and the like. However, bear in mind that routine maintenance, including painting must be done while the rooms are vacant and prior to the following academic year. With the ongoing maintenance issues, I would be very surprised if any company would rent the building on a full FRI lease, knowing how many repairs have to be carried out on an annual basis when letting to students.

– New student block let to a specialist student company - 50 rooms plus - over 10 years until expiration, on full FRI national covenant: 6.5%

– Student block, let direct to students by landlord assuming 80% occupancy, 10 years old plus - under 50 rooms covenant:15%

– New purpose-built block let to a national covenant, FRI 10 years: 6% yield

– Converted accommodation let to a local covenant, FRI 5 to 10 years: 8.5% yield

SELF-STORAGE

This type of investment has become very popular over the last few years and there are a few national companies that have purpose-built self-storage sites across the UK. Additionally, there are a few owner-run operations and I even know a few property investors who have seen the potential income these can produce and run them themselves, rather than leasing them out to a third party.

At the other end of the scale, there are people who will try and manage this type of investment on the cheap. There are currently a number of farm-type buildings that look dreadful, and offer very cheap, and unprofessionally run storage, many based in areas with poor road and access links.

My brother, Edward, has four self-storage centres in different parts of the UK and runs them very successfully. He leases the buildings and then creates the self-storage units to let out on a monthly basis. He tells me that, in some cases, he stores people's personal belongings for years - I really don't quite understand why anyone would do that. On the other hand, I can completely understand if you're moving to a new home that is not ready, you would need to use this type of storage. He tells me he had one client who would visit his storage unit every Sunday morning in order to sit down and read the Sunday papers!

Compared to America, pro-rata, we have very little self-storage in the UK, so I think there is room for growth in this sector of the market. Interestingly, the banks seem to like this type of investment, no doubt as they feel there is safety in numbers and if you're renting to literally hundreds of different people on a monthly basis, they are not all going to suddenly give notice and remove their belongings. So, whether you're looking to purchase a building to rent it out to a self-storage operator, or you're looking to run it yourself, there seems great demand depending, as always, on the location.

- Purpose-built warehouse let to a national covenant, FRI 10 years: 6% yield

- Converted building let to a local covenant, FRI 5 to 10 years: 9%

In outlining these different types of investment properties with examples, I hope that they are helpful in your decision-making when it comes to what you would like to invest in, and what yield you can expect to get. In the next chapter, I'll focus on how you go about receiving your rent and what happens when you don't.

CHAPTER 10
RENT PAYMENTS

The way you receive your rent payments depends on the type of lease, and any other negotiations you may have had with your tenants. Typically, with any commercial lease, the rent is payable three months in advance. This arrangement gives you the confidence that your tenant has the money to continue paying the rent and is great for cash flow. Also, if they are unable to pay the three months rent at a time, this gives you an early heads-up, and the time to plan accordingly.

Most full repairing and insuring leases contain a clause that in the event of the rent not being paid within a month of the due date, you can instruct bailiffs to go in and take possessions up to the value of any rent due. This is a great deterrent, and something I have threatened to use on occasions with some of the larger tenants in my portfolio, but as of the time of writing, it's not something I have ever gone through with.

The consequences of instructing bailiffs in that matter, are that once you have 'entered' the premises, they could potentially hand back their keys and have no further financial commitment to the lease they signed. Not all leases will have this clause, so when you purchase an investment property you must have your solicitor thoroughly read the lease so that you fully understand what you can and cannot do to collect the rent.

I'd like to take this opportunity to point out, some solicitors are, frankly, better than others. You may be inheriting a lease that is either poorly written, or less favourable to yourself as the landlord.

After you have purchased an investment property, you may find that you are unable to collect rent three months in advance. Very few tenants would chose to pay you in advance if they do not need to. You should not rely on the terms of the rent payment, or any other terms, changing in the lease after you have purchased it.

If, you later get to the point of negotiating a new lease with the existing tenant, you could still run into difficulty. If the current lease is within the Landlord and Tenant Act 1954, this requires you to offer the tenant a lease on similar terms to the one which has just expired.

Clearly, with a new tenant, everything is up for negotiation! However, trying to get three months rent in advance from a local shop is probably not realistic. In this case, it may be best to consider accepting rent monthly within the terms of the new lease.

When considering the terms that you want in the lease, you must consider who your tenant is and set realistic and doable targets. There is no advantage in signing a lease which is highly favourable but completely unsuited to the property and the parties involved.

In 2020, when COVID struck, I was far more concerned about my commercial tenants than my residential ones. Everyone needs a roof over their heads, and most of my residential tenants paid in full. If only this were the case with the commercial ones too! Some of my tenants are consistently late with payments, and generally hard work, but COVID gave them an excuse for no payment. Some, like countless businesses throughout the UK, were faced with very real financial difficulty.

Throughout my career, I have been proud to have some national covenants within my commercial portfolio. Having the larger tenants offers some peace of mind, in the event that the local shop tenants cannot pay for one reason or another, these bigger ones will always pay the rent on time and on a quarterly basis.

It was in 2020 that I realised my foolishness. Within a week of the COVID lockdown, I had calls from three of my national tenants telling me that they were not going to pay the rent, and forcibly suggesting that they should be given a six-month rent-free period to account for their inability to open their doors. However, I, like many other landlords, had mortgages to pay on these properties.

Some of these national tenants had over 100 outlets each and had probably said the same to all their landlords. I sat and considered the problem, and decided to do nothing but let it play out. My logic was that if some of the other landlords panicked and agreed to these terms, the tenants could then afford to pay me my full rent when it was due.

In their wisdom, the Government decided to not allow any commercial evictions from premises where rent was owed. This gave every rogue tenant the opportunity of a lifetime to accept the help offered by the government, in terms of the rate-free period, grants available and the Bounce Back loans – many of which, in my opinion, will never be repaid. However, they offered no help for the landlords whatsoever, even though I would think that almost all landlords in the country vote Conservative!

I stuck to my guns, and surprise, surprise, they paid their rent on time. This was presumably because they had managed to reduce their rent burden by numerous landlords agreeing to their terms. I hope this is a good demonstration of standing your ground, even when it comes to the bigger companies. Don't let them bully you into accepting lesser terms than those legally agreed!

The policy that I made up on the hoof during the pandemic within my commercial portfolio was that, financially speaking, if the tenant were bigger than me, I would expect the full rent. However, if they were financially smaller than me, I was willing to help in any way I could to keep the tenants in situ so that I didn't have a vacant unit on my hands when the world began to reopen.

I'm not quite sure whether this policy has really worked, because in some cases I have had properties where I couldn't even get hold of the tenants for nine months or more, even when I know that they would have received financial support from the government.

I would like to clarify, that when I say 'help in any way I could', I do not mean writing the rent off. The rent is still owed, and some of my tenants are still paying it off to this day. In many cases, I have now agreed to receive rent monthly, even where the lease state quarterly, but I took the view that at least I am still getting it, rather than pushing them and the tenant walks away.

The reason the yields are higher than with other tenants is due to their ability to pay rent in the event of financial difficulty. The smaller the trader, in general, the less likely they are to be able to weather any significant storms. However, the last thing any landlord wants or needs is a vacant premises where they are liable for rates, whilst also needing to continue paying their mortgage to the bank.

My message to you with regards to rent collection is to be firm but fair. You should support the weaker tenants by adjusting when the rent is due, if needed you can collect rent monthly rather than quarterly. You need to keep your tenants, unless you are confident that you can relet very quickly.

The key to maintaining a relationship with your tenants is to maintain a good line of communication. Show an interest in the building and ask how business is going for them. Ultimately, some of the smaller premises, especially lock-up shops, are working for you as landlords, as there isn't much profit left after they have paid rent and rates. Where possible, I do my very best to meet my tenants, shake their hand, and have a cup of tea with them. The better your relationship with your tenant, the more likely they are to prioritise paying you.

As soon as a tenant is late with rent, I personally contact them to ask what the problem is. Many of them will open up and explain their problem. I always say it's much easier to deal with the problem head-on rather than bury your head in the sand. You don't want to let the problem get to a stage where it can't be ignored, and you need to evict them because there isn't an alternative solution.

Sometimes, you have to reduce rent in the short term where necessary, but they are made aware that the rent is due when things improve.

Next, I'd like to give some advice on what to do when a tenant is in arrears. As I'm sure you're aware, I am not a lawyer and this is my opinion. You should consult your solicitor and take their legal advice.

FORFEITURE OF LEASE

Within most commercial leases their will be a forfeiture of lease clause, allowing the landlord to forfeit the lease if a tenant breaks certain conditions, usually including non-payment of rent or insurance over a specific period. Once the tenant has broken these conditions, you as a landlord must act quickly to forfeit the lease, otherwise it is deemed that they have waived the right to do so.

Earlier in the chapter, I mentioned arranging for the late payment of rent. This is likely to be viewed as an act of waiver. Therefore, you should be aware that you may want to act quickly and instruct a bailiff to get your property back. For many landlords, including myself, this is the very last option, as once you have possession you need to relet the property.

In the event of your tenant going into either administration or receivership, the administrator has the right to forfeit the lease within 28 days. This is a nightmare scenario for a landlord if you consider that there is likely a lot of rent owed.

You may also hear that a Pre-Pack Agreement has been reached, this is when the sale of the business is agreed prior to the appointment of administrators. In this case, they will approach the landlord to get the agreement through to reduce the rent going forward. The landlord is left with choosing the least worst option. If they don't accept a rent reduction then the business will likely go into administration and they are left with no tenant in that property.

RENT COLLECTION

Now we are thoroughly depressed about all the ways things can go wrong, let's take a look on the bright side for those of you still looking to become a landlord; collecting rent.

You need to decide how you wish to collect the rent from your tenants. For many years, I have used a commercial management company. These companies usually charge between 4% and 10%, depending on the size of your portfolio, but they will tackle the day to day issues that arise, giving you some freedom. The management companies also keep an eye on when leases are up for renewal or rent review.

Although, in more recent times, I have managed some of my portfolio myself through my business manager, David Marsh. I am exceptionally lucky to have someone of his skill working with me.

I'd also like to point out that should you be fortunate enough to have any national, or even international, tenants, they are probably the easiest tenants to manage in normal times. This is because they are very large organisations and are usually able to pay rent on time.

Sometimes these tenants will even tell you when the rent review is due, as they will either have their own estates departments, or they have their own commercial property agency advising them on a regular basis.

CHAPTER 11
FUNDING COMMERCIAL PROPERTY

For many years, the way that residential or commercial property was funded was very similar. The main clearing banks on the high street would lend around 50% loan-to-value for purchasing and developing residential properties, and it was similar for any commercial investment, provided the rent cover was 100%. For example, if the rent was £20,000 per annum, the repayment on the mortgage couldn't be any more than £10,000. Interestingly, this hasn't really changed at all in the commercial sector.

However, for residential funding, there has been dramatic changes, particularly for what lenders consider an acceptable LTV (loan-to-value). Thousands of small property banks have opened up and are now lending to inexperienced investors making it incredibly easy to enter the residential investment market.

Many of these same inexperienced investors are still unable to purchase commercial property because of the requirements of the banks requiring a maximum loan to value of 50%.

The differences in the way commercial and residential property is funded puts commercial property at a huge disadvantage when we consider it's value when vacant. At my seminars, I often ask "what do you think would happen to residential property values if you could only get a 50% loan to value?" I get answers that range from, no difference at all to a reduction in value of 30%. I think the latter is probably closer to the correct answer.

So you can extrapolate my theory here to what has happened to the value of vacant commercial property, particularly in high streets throughout the UK. I would even argue that it's closer to 50% reduction in value in some cases. For example, I am currently buying a very large building in decent condition for £38 per square foot, where as the cost of building new would be £200 per square foot. Why has this happened? Well, rent has halved, and as I explained at the start, the value is based on yield.

To make things even more difficult for the would be commercial investor, unless you have a a track record or strong financial backing, many banks will not even entertain offering a loan on vacant commercial property. This gives the rest of us even more opportunity to purchase at huge discounts.

However, they still need to be funded and ultimately let, so to whom will these banks lend, and at what percentage?

The first thing to say is, even if you have a good relationship with a major high street bank and substantial funds, they are extremely slow at dealing with applications. For most investors, it's a complete waste of time to go to them for any sort of commercial loan. They say they're in the business of lending, but my experience has been that this is for a select few and that they are difficult to deal with.

So, who does that leave? The thousands of residential property lenders I mentioned earlier will normally run a mile from lending on vacant commercial property. However, there are a select number of smaller banks that will lend on commercial property, up to 50 or 60% of the loan to the value given the right investor. The right investor is one who has a plan of action and a report from a commercial surveyor to support their figures.

When presenting a vacant building to the bank, I always ensure that I have the advice and report from a chartered commercial surveyor to back up what I'm saying. If the property is let, most banks will lend for the length of least that you have in place. So, if you have a ten-year lease on a shop, they will lend you the money over a term of ten years, on the basis that loan repayments are covered 100% by the rent. This will likely limit you to getting an interest-only loan on the property, as with repayments, it's likely to exceed the banking mandate of 100% cover.

If there residential accommodation above, which is let out separately, then most banks will take this into account and accept it as a much safer rent flow. In other words, if all residential tenants were to vacate, you can relet them more easily than the commercial space. On this basis, the bank may not require as much as 100% rent cover. On purely commercial investments, I don't seem to manage to borrow more than 50% loan to value. The good thing about this is that you won't be financially overstretched, as long as the tenant remains in place.

Regarding leisure tenants, for example nightclubs, then potentially you'll be paying more interest, and if it's a short lease your loan may be declined. To the bank, it's all about risk. Risk is also important for landlords, the difference being that banks won't take any!

For those of you with a mixed portfolio or with additional collateral, the bank will then look at a vacant commercial building more positively. They may potentially ask for a personal guarantee, which, if your statement of assets is adequate, they may consider lending on vacant commercial property.

Back in 2008, I felt particularly relaxed, having no personal guarantees with any banks at all. By the middle of 2009, the banks began to panic about the market, and I had to offer substantial guarantees for them to continue supporting my investments. A crazy situation when you consider that I was only geared to 50% LTV. Since then, I have managed to reduce the guarantees needed.

Another constraint that many banks are now trying to enforce is insisting on a debenture on the limited company taking out the loan. This limits the company because no other bank will lend it money while that debenture is in place. The bank with the debenture has security over all company assets, whether they have a charge on them or not.

If you're looking to borrow money from another bank with a debenture in place, the simplest way around this is to lend any cash funds in the company to a new company that you set up. You then use that company with a loan to go to the bank and purchase further property. That way, the original bank that holds the debenture over the original company, has no financial control over the new company.

If you are looking to invest in commercial property for the first time, I advise you to contact a good commercial finance broker. They will be able to advise you of the banks in the current marketplace, including the level at which they will lend and to whom. They normally charge a percentage fee for their services if they find you a mortgage.

CHAPTER 12
BUYING VACANT COMMERCIAL PROPERTY

If you can fund it, I honestly believe that there has never been a better time to buy vacant commercial property. There are amazing opportunities out there, and some of these buildings would cost five times more to build than you can buy them for, and that doesn't include the cost of the land.

Currently, I'm making a real effort to purchase some of these large commercial buildings, often in town centre locations. Do not believe all the talk around towns and cities being dead and that nobody wants to shop there or trade from them. Of course, I believe that the high street is changing, but this is the time when investors and developers can take advantage of the negativity in the marketplace.

In the future, the high street will have a different feel, more residential accommodation and fewer shops, open spaces, and quality housing. I take this opportunity to point out that I have noticed the smaller market towns performing better than the big towns and city centres. There has been a real desire to support local shops where people live rather than drive to larger shopping complexes. This, in turn, has stabilised commercial rents in these spaces, unlike high streets throughout the UK.

Local authorities have been burying their head in the sand for many years now, trying to retain as many commercial buildings as possible. If I were cynical, I might suggest this is due to the huge amount of money raised by commercial rates.

An example of this is Debenhams. All of their stores have now closed, but I know that one of their stores were paying £500,000 in rates, and I would imagine this was a roundabout figure for many of their stores.

The Government has now taken notice of councils not allowing commercial property to be converted to other uses. It's a disgrace really that it has needed the Government stepping in to do the job that should have been done by every local planning authority. It's now been taken out of the local planning authority hands and permitted development rights (see chapter 13) have been forced through in most councils. Local councils aren't pleased to have lost control of this process, and in some cases are doing whatever they can to resist it being allowed in their area.

There are clearly far too many commercial shops in our towns and cities, and until many are converted into other uses, predominantly residential, rent levels will remain low compared to what they were ten years ago. I know of buildings that were once let for £100,000 per annum, and now the landlord would be happy to accept £35,000 per annum.

When you hear about the way that rent prices have reduced, you might be wondering why invest in commercial property? But all of this just reiterates my point that there are tremendous opportunities to purchase vacant commercial property at massive discounts. People will tell you that there are not tenants, but there are for shops in the right areas if you can rent them competitively.

You can afford to rent them competitively when you're purchasing at a discounted rate. Not only that, but you're also thinking about rent levels that allow retailers to make profits, meaning that you can hopefully retain them for many years to come.

I have been quite surprised by the number of tenants that are looking for new premises, even with this being a very difficult time for many retailers. They are out there if you can offer up the right rental package, and perhaps being flexible with rent changes, stepping up to the level you believe it should be over time.

I like to purchase bigger vacant commercial properties, ones that you can split up into two or three different units. That way, even if I can't let the whole ground floor, I should be able to let one or two smaller units. I'm constantly looking at how I can de-risk my future investments, and splitting up the commercial space, or converting to residential on the upper floors is a great way.

Also, please don't forget that even if the building is vacant you will have empty rate, unless the building is listed. I talk more about historical buildings and the associated challenges in Chapter 14.

You should be aware that insurance can be an issue with a vacant commercial space, with many insurers not wishing to take the risk on empty buildings, or charging much higher premiums. You should make sure you investigate all insurance issues prior to the exchange of contracts.

CHAPTER 13
DEVELOPING UNDER PERMITTED DEVELOPMENT RIGHTS

Permitted development rights (PD) has been around in one form or another for many years. In 2013, the Government's frustration at the lack of planning permission to allow the conversion of commercial office space to residential property brought about permitted developments rights, thereby allowing offices to be converted to residential use – to the annoyance of virtually every local authority. England alone requires approximately 500,000 new homes to be built every year to cope with the housing demand. On average, the current number of new homes is less than half of this, so you can see why the Government was determined to drive this through.

PD rights removed the need for a full planning application for change of use from offices to residential. Instead, the applicant needs to put plans in to the local authority, which then has 56 days to either issue a licence or refuse them to develop the property. The government went even further, stipulating that if a decision has not been made on an application within 56 days, then it would be deemed that permission had been granted.

Further still, under the new law, at the time of writing there is no current requirement for social housing which is required if more than 1000 sq m is to be developed for residential accommodation. However, this could very well change and is predicted to. Usually, a third of all units must be for social housing if the property is over 1000 m², but sometimes this can be up to 50% of units.

There used to be only a few reasons why the local authority could turn down the application. One reason was if there were adequate cycle stores, typically one cycle space per flat, but no vehicle parking was required. Also, there needed to be space for bin storage and adequate natural light. There was no limit on the size of each self-contained unit and there were no requirements to make any changes to the external appearance of the building.

Many investors benefitted from the lack of size constraints for each self contained unit by cramming as many 'micro units' into a building as possible. Some were done well, and were marketed to young professionals who were happy with the finished product, but some were developed poorly and let to the most vulnerable in our society. The latter has caused huge social problems in some of these blocks, the largest I am aware of is over 250 units in one building.

If I were a buy-to-let investor, in one of these large blocks which have been poorly converted without external renovations, I would be very concerned about my investment. You can see them appearing now in auctions with very low reserves. I would also be nervous about investing in PD schemes converted above commercial units. These are definitely the cheapest new apartment investments, particularly when there are restaurants or take-aways below. There are not many lending institutions that will lend on a flat above food outlets.

Some architects have described these cheap conversions that lack external aesthetics as "the slums of the futures", and while I often disagree with architects and their reluctance to save money where possible, I must agree with them on this occasion.

Commercial agents were very slow to recognise the potential of converting office buildings into residential use under the scheme, and this meant that a lot of offices were purchased at a good price by the early adopters, and many millions were made as a result.

As with most fruitful opportunities, the returns diminish over time. With so many new developers coming into the market, and this type of commercial to residential development being one that people can cut their teeth on, the market has become saturated with people willing to pay more than the professional developers are willing to pay.

Moreover, from August 2021, the permitted development rules were widened to include some small shops and modest extensions. Developers are now required to prove that parking is not necessary and meet a number of other new restrictions.

If you have a building that is detached there is a possibility of going up two extra floors under the scheme. However, the planning office reserves the right to refuse permission if they don't like the external look of the building, or if it overlooked by other properties. To my mind, this gives them the ability to turn down just about anything that suits them, especially in built up areas.

There was also an announcement to allow PD rights for change of use from Class E to residential. This very important change to the town and country planning 'Use Class Order' of 1987 was in September 2020 when Class E was introduced, and this Class now covers the former use classes of A1 (shops), A2 (financial and professional), A3 (restaurants), and parts of D1 (non-residential institutions) as well as D2, which includes some leisure.

This is clearly a huge change and gives commercial investors the flexibility and opportunity, if they can't let their shop or other commercial properties that now come under class E, to convert to residential use, whether it is to retain or sell. However, I would point out that many shops do not convert very well for residential use, and you may find it difficult to sell to owner-occupiers. So, in many cases, I think you must assume once converted the property needs to remain as a residential investment rather than sold off to the residential market.

Some developers are cleverly getting around the rules legally and creating more ground floor rear space that they are then converting to residential while keeping the shop at the front.

If you live in London this is particularly good news because the cost of any small apartment will probably be a lot more than the cost of converting the building. However, if you're based outside London, in certain areas, especially up north, there will be little point in conversion as the cost of converting will be as much as the new flat is worth.

Although the government has done its best to increase the flexibility and opportunity for commercial landlords to be able to convert to residential with a PD, they've also allowed and made it easier for tenants and landlords alike who wish to change the use of an existing commercial building.

Many years ago, it was difficult to obtain planning permission. For example for an office, in the town centre, I'd have to submit planning applications in order for permission for "change of use" from a shop to an estate agency. Sometimes, without success, which when you think back now, is crazy. The council's argument was that they wanted to retain retail in the town centres and therefore, did not encourage travel agents and estate agents. The landscape has clearly changed, and as always, the local authority is so far behind the times that it was necessary for the government to step in and do something about it.

So, although these new rules are very useful, councils have been given more legal reason to turn down PD applications than they had, up until the new changes. They have also become more expert in arguing their cases against more well-informed planning consultants.

To counter these new rules, councils are somewhat controversially using Article 4, which is for protecting the appearance of conservation areas. This allows the council to stop certain activities in an area, a common example being disallowing any further homes of multiple occupation without a full planning application in a certain area of a town or city.

Now, Article 4 was not designed, and never should be used to stop permitted development in my view, and I won't be surprised if the government does something about this, as it's becoming more and more evident that local authorities are using this means to stop permitted development.

This, of course, does not stop you from putting in a full application on any development that is within an Article 4 area, but I would assume because the local authority has designated it as such, you are unlikely to be granted planning permission. If you do succeed via the normal planning application route, you will have other costs to incur before you can proceed with the development. These costs might include the provision of social housing if over 1,000 sqm, possibly a contribution towards open space areas, and provision of school places. The list these days can be endless!

I would now like to point out that just because you can develop a building into residential use, this doesn't mean you always should. For instance, if you're buying a building in a very commercial area, I would question whether developing flats would be the best solution. If you need finance to develop the scheme, are possibly looking to refinance the development at the end, or sell the flats, the question you should be asking yourself is, "Who is going to rent or purchase them?". The question I always ask myself is, "Would I want a daughter of mine to live there?" If the answer is no, then I'm always very cautious of development.

You will find many people who will give you advice about the possibility of whether you can get permitted development on a scheme. I have lost count of the number of estate agents and commercial agents who have told me that permitted development won't be a problem on the building they are selling. Personally, there is only one person I ask and that's my planning consultant, and I recommend that you find a good one and do the same. The rules are very complicated, and a clever planning consultant can either make you a lot of money or save you from losing a lot of money.

Ultimately, if you can apply for PD for residential, between getting your offer accepted and purchasing the property, on the basis that it shouldn't take longer than 56 days, then that has got to be the very safest way forward. If you don't want to go to that expense, I suggest you put in a pre-application to the council, along with plans showing what you wish to do to the building, and hopefully you will get a positive response.

Under the current rules, the planning department should come back to you within 30 working days, although many take longer. If you can do either of the above before you exchange, you will sleep better. As I say, property development is all about avoiding risking the deal as much as possible before you have even purchased the property.

CHAPTER 14

LISTED BUILDINGS & CONSERVATION AREAS

LISTED BUILDINGS

Listed buildings are those considered to have historical importance: there are over 400,000 of these in England and there are three levels, Grade II, Grade II*, and Grade I. Since 2012, there has been an increase of 18% of listed buildings being occupied for commercial purposes and there are now around 12,000 listed buildings which have a commercial purpose, although I am surprised there aren't more.

Historic England is a charity and the Government's statutory advisor on the historic environment. Historic England champions these historic spaces, and educates people on the value and how we can care for them.

Now, let us consider the ways in which the three grades differ, beginning with Grade II. This is the easiest Grade in terms of getting permission to make internal changes. However, as with all other listed buildings there is very little chance of being able to make changes that affect the external appearance of a Grade II listed building.

For example, if you are seeking to put a doorway on the ground floor to add to the existing shop door, to create independent access to the first and second floors, you have virtually no chance in my experience. However, if there is a rear entrance, you may be able to use the existing staircase to separate the ground and upper floors. This is something I have done on numerous occasions.

Either a conservation officer or a listed building officer (if available) at the local authority is the best person to advise you on what is possible. I urge you to take their advice prior to purchasing the property. Do not think you can steam in there making all sorts of changes without listed building consent, otherwise you will find yourself in serious legal trouble.

Grade II* is even more of a challenge. It has a higher level of historical importance but is functionally similar to Grade II. You may well be able to block up certain areas that you don't wish to be exposed, but any changes you make must be done in a way that allows you to restore the property to it's original state in the future.

If you need to strip out a Grade II* listed building to begin restoration, then I implore you to photograph and document everything that you remove, and to leave it on the premises until permission, (even if only verbally), has been given that it is not of historical interest. If there is a very nice fireplace in situ, don't even think about taking it out and putting it in your own home, you will be arrested!

Finally, there is Grade I listed. I have only ever converted two of these buildings and am fairly confident I have no desire to do another. Grade I listed properties are those of exceptional historical or architectural importance, and therefore have the strictest conditions imposed upon their preservation. I was offered a Grade I listed investment property in Chester recently. It had some very good, well-known tenants on long leases. But, I noticed that they were only on internal repairing and insuring leases, unsurprising considering any work to repair or renew the façade of a Grade I listed building can be very expensive. I'm certain that very few tenants would want to undertake the responsibility of a Grade I listed building's external.

Therein are the two main challenges with any listed building: the cost of repairing it in order to let it in the first place and maintaining the building to a good standard. This will put off most investors. Although, this can be an advantage because it may mean you end up with an investment on a better yield. However, this is a risky strategy, and you need to accept that should you wish to sell it, there won't be many potential buyers. Importantly, unless it really is a landmark building, it will be a challenge to find tenants to occupy the building – particularly on a FRI lease.

I recognise that this may all seem quite negative, but there are certainly some positives associated with listed buildings. Firstly, listed buildings mean there are no empty rates payable. Secondly, sometimes there is the possibility of obtaining a grant for the restoration of a listed buildings. These grants are normally made available by the local authority, but are spent quickly after the start of the financial year in April. So, if you're seeking one, I recommend getting your application in as early in the financial year as you can. Thirdly, some investors are not VAT registered, but there is the opportunity to pay less VAT on certain works for listed buildings, but I recommend you take advice from your VAT consultant on this.

CONSERVATION AREA

If a building is not listed but is in a conservation area it can also present challenges with regards to the external façade.

I was recently involved in a commercial development in Southwold, a beautiful coastal town, and popular with holidaymakers. We purchased a building that was a residential property in the high street and needed to change the residential windows to full-length shop windows. However, this was turned down due to it being in a conservation area. We then sought to change the front door from a residential style to a glass one, not thinking the local authority would take issue with it. Once again, they refused us. We were forced to let the building for less rent than we hoped, having been unable to undertake some alterations.

In some conservation areas, you may not encounter these same problems, and it will vary depending on the guidance in different areas. However, this is a cautionary tale based on our experience in the beautiful town of Southwold. So, if you wish to make alterations, I recommend checking with the local authority.

All in all, I wouldn't advise against you buying a listed building as an investment, I have some in my own portfolio. This is more a warning to mindful about the yield because you are likely to need to outlay some money in the future for repairs to the fabric of the building. Anybody that currently lives in a listed country house, and I do, can attest to this being a constant commitment.

CHAPTER 15
FINANCIAL LEVERAGE

One of the factors that makes residential property such a popular investment is that they can be leveraged for such a high loan to value. For example, you could buy a property for £100,000, refurbish it, and have it revalued at £150,000, and then get back all the cash you initially invested, and use this to find another similar deal.

However, as we discussed earlier in the book, to finance a commercial property at more than a 50% loan to value is quite a challenge. Although, this doesn't mean you cannot use the same tactic for commercial that you use for residential. In fact, the level at which you can leverage could be much greater; this is on the basis that when you buy a vacant property, you're buying it at a much lower level in the current market.

The market value of a vacant commercial property, compared to one that is let on a full FRI lease can be extraordinary. For example, some years ago I bought a parade of part vacant shops in Dovercourt, Essex. Part of the building, designed as a small supermarket, had never been occupied in over 20 years. I purchased this property during the 1992 recession and let it on a temporary basis as an indoor market, which saved me from paying the empty rates. Another option to avoid empty rates is to let it to a charity, which may even pay reduced rent on a temporary basis if you aren't feeling very charitable.

One day, I got a phone call from Ewan Dodds, who owns a company called Whybrows in Colchester and is a very successful commercial agent. He said to me, "What would be the best ever news I could give you today, John?" I replied, "That you have let the building being used as the indoor market." He replied, "I've done better than that. I've let it to the Job Centre. They will take a 20-year lease, with five-yearly reviews, and are going to spend £250,000 fitting out the office."

Now, on that basis, not only was I able to refinance with the bank and get the original cash back that I had invested into the parade, but also an extra £210,000 on the back of the fact that I'd let the indoor market to the Job Centre, part of the government. Now there are blue chip tenants and then, there's the government!

I do appreciate that this is a slightly exaggerated example, but this successful letting gives you an example of how a decent lease, ideally ten years or more, will enable the refinance of the building; at least, getting the money that was originally invested back and putting it into the next investment deal. Not only will you have retained the property, got your original cash investment back, but will also have surplus cash every quarter from the rent received, over and above your bank repayments.

This is how people have built up large investment portfolios up and down the UK. When you can refinance each new property purchase once it's let, the easier it becomes time after time. The point will come when the bank isn't quite so difficult with regards to the type of tenants in your portfolio and will at look the overall rental income as a business. This will give you more flexibility to purchase slightly more challenging opportunities going forward.

CHAPTER 16
BUYING COMMERCIAL PROPERTY AT AUCTION

Many commercial properties now find themselves in a public auction. Apart from it being an excellent way to sell this type of property, it has likely been offered up by a commercial agent on the open market for some time, and the owner has got fed up waiting for it to be sold. Often, sales have been agreed, only for them to fall through.

I've been buying and selling at auction for 35 years, and in 2009, along with my business partner, I purchased a large shareholding in Auction House UK. I was proud of our role in making it into the biggest, predominantly residential, property auction business in the country by volume of properties sold annually. We then sold our shares in 2018. I've since written a book about auctions, which I would recommend if you were considering purchasing at auction. I believe auction to be a fantastic way of buying property at a discounted price.

My first recommendation when purchasing at auction; you need to know why the property is there. Sometimes it's obvious, other times there is a hidden reason, either way, you need to know what that is. Other than speaking to the auctioneer, and hoping they will be honest with you, you can also speak to neighbours and find out what they know. It never ceases to amaze me how much knowledge a neighbour has, and how much they are willing to share, particularly about why a property is still on the market, and how many times a sale has fallen through.

Once you've established why the property is for sale, you should then download the legal pack, which can be found on the auctioneer's website. You should get this straight to your solicitor, as they will be able to advise on any legal problems.

If the property is occupied, you need to understand what is in the lease, how long it has left to run, whether or not there is an upward-only rent review, whether it's within the 1954 act and so on. There is nothing more frustrating than buying a commercial property on a 10% yield, producing £50,000 per annum, only for this to be reduced to £30,000 per annum on a rent review shortly after purchase.

Often, legal packs are not entirely complete. Sometimes, the solicitor has not had enough time to produce all the information required for a legal pack prior to auction. Vendors often forget how much time is required to get the local search carried out, for instance. Or, perhaps they've owned the property for a long time, and can't find the deeds. Either way, the information that is missing could be just as important as what you have in front of you.

It is vital that you read the special conditions of sale of the property that you are interested in, this will be available from the auctioneer. Ensure that you read the information unique to the property you are bidding on and read it thoroughly prior to the start of the auction. You also should be aware that there may be a buyer's premium, and you need to know how much this is, because it can vary from £500 to thousands. A buyers premium is normally a percentage amount and will be paid by the purchaser on top of the winning bid.

Another vital question is whether there are any rent arrears. Some auctioneers will direct you back to the legal pack and others will be more forthcoming. A trick often employed by vendors, is to get purchasers to pay the rent arrears owed to them by tenants.

I purchased my first commercial property at auction in 1983, and it was certainly a learning curve. I did everything wrong. I didn't check the legal pack, I had not viewed the property, and there was a clause in the contract meaning I had to pay any rent arrears. You can learn from my mistakes here.

Occasionally, even by auction day the legal pack will not be complete, and in this instance, you should take your solicitors advice. It may be that they have deliberately left out vital information because it is detrimental to the sale. Remember, when you're buying at auction, it's 'buyer beware'.

The last four commercial properties I have acquired have been purchased after the auction, when they haven't sold in the room, or via the internet as the case sometimes is now. It's also no coincidence that all four properties were in the hands of receivers as the current owners had gone bankrupt.

Auctions are usually an early indicator of market trends, with the general market following what is happening at auction with a delay of about six to nine months. The auction market is the barometer and the sharp end of the industry.

If you are serious about buying at auction, then I recommend joining the EIG (Essential Information Group), allowing you to access information about every auction taking place in the UK, and inform you of what properties have not sold. It's a great way to gain insight into the current market.

EIG is still run by David Sandeman, who started the business many years ago. I've know David for a long time, and consider him a walking encyclopaedia of auction statistics. I was delighted when he agreed to write the foreword for my book 'Buying & Selling Property At Auction'.

The clearance rate for an auction, or the number of lots sold, normally sits around 70%, sometimes 50% in a tough market. Auctioneers do not include all the properties that are in the auction catalogue within this figure. For example if a property is withdrawn from the market it will not factor into this number. More importantly, if the property doesn't receive a single bid at the auction then it does not count towards the statistics either.

It is my view, that so long as you are careful, you view the property, take my advice and the legal opinion of your solicitor, there is no reason not to purchase at auction. Normally, you can expect less competition than on the open market, with a realistic reserve.

You must make sure you have your funds organised to purchase. If the hammer falls, and you pay your 10%, the next 28 days running around trying to find a bank that will lend you the money to complete will be very stressful. I can't count the number of people who tell me about when they went to their first auction, with no plan of bidding on a property, who then got excited, put their hand up and became the proud owner of a property, without the proper research on that lot or their funds in place!

This has happened to both first-time auction goers and experience investors alike, so you need to make sure you aren't one of them. Be aware, there is no legal way of withdrawing from the purchase. When the hammer comes down, you legally own the property and have 28 days in which to complete. Whilst it is usually 28 days, I have also known it to be as much as six weeks, and as little as 20 days.

CHAPTER 17
RENTING OUT VACANT SPACE

I am always amazed that some investors with a vacant space will just hand this over to a commercial agent for rent, and after months still demonstrate no flexibility on their lease terms, offering no encouragement to any potential tenant.

I have a joint venture fund, which is predominantly used by first-time developers, putting up the junior debt in return for a 50% share of the profit. I guide them through the whole process, making the development as successful as possible. My mantra is always "let's make it happen", and that's exactly what you must remember when you have a vacant commercial premises.

No matter how good your agent is, you cannot rely on them to do all of the work. You are the captain of your ship, and you are the one who is making the decisions on whether you want to accept a reduced rent or a shorter lease.

Let me tell you about some of the methods I've employed over the years to facilitate the letting of my properties as quickly as possible. The first and obvious one really is the rent-free period. Now, this can be abused by many new tenants going into premises To stop the tenant from getting a six months' rent-free period and then running off when it doesn't work, I make them commit to at least the first quarter's rent in advance. They get the six months' rent-free period and then they start paying normally, in advance, on a quarterly basis.

Another method is to stagger the rent, so it reaches the level I want within the first three years. For example, if I want £40,000 per annum, but they are a new business, I might offer them a rent-free period to get them off to a good start, particularly if they are paying for the fit out. The rent might then start out at £30,000 for the first year, £35,000 for the second, and reaching the full £40,000 for the third year.

What some investors do here is have their tenant sign the lease at the full rental figure of £40,000 from the start of the lease, and then give them a side letter to confirm the rent reduction for the first two years. While it is not something I would ever recommend, but does happen, they may then keep the side letter private and not inform the bank's valuer when refinancing.

I cannot recall a time when I haven't needed to give a rent-free period at the start of a lease, even if it's only for the first quarter. Most tenants will ask for a rent-free period to give them time to fit out the new shop. I mentioned earlier that I have a Chinese restaurant wishing to go into a new vacant commercial building that I own. They are a small enterprise and it would be a deal-breaker should the tenant have to pay for the full fit out, and cost of the commercial kitchen. In this instance, I think the best option is to support them in this if I want to get the property let.

Although I am normally quite happy to allow a rent free period, I'm not normally so keen to put actual cash into a building, even though you can argue these improvements benefit me as a landlord if the tenant were to leave the property. Before I commit to ploughing cash into the fit out, I need to see a financial commitment from the incoming tenant. I need to retain as much cash as possible for my next investment purchase.

One thing I always try to avoid, is allowing too many changes from the tenant to the lease that was drafted by my solicitor. This is because your lease needs to be watertight to make the property as mortgageable as possible. When a surveyor comes to value the property, they will want to look at the lease. If you have conceded too many major points, it's too loose, or you've been too flexible with some of the terms, they won't consider this to be a watertight lease. For example, if your tenant had a survey done and found the roof to be in poor condition, so you relieve them of their responsibility for maintaining it, that would weaken your lease. Instead, what I would do is pay for the roof to be repaired, then they sign the lease inclusive of them taking responsibility for this.

You must always be thinking of how to protect the value of your investment regarding revaluations and increases in the capital value. This may mean that you have to invest more of your own capital prior to the lease being signed, but you then have a far more watertight lease.

These days, you will find smaller potential tenants who don't want to commit to more than three years on a lease. I even had one recently who only wanted to commit to one year! This to me, is a complete waste of time. Even if I'm happy with the rent level, how am I going to be able to refinance and move onto my next deal with only one year of rental security? If you really must accept this type of deal, I would try to get the tenant to sign a longer lease with a break clause after the first year. It's better than the property being vacant, and hopefully they do well and don't need to trigger the break clause.

One of the major challenges when letting a property can be your tenant's solicitor. They can take a very long time negotiating with your solicitors, and in the meantime, you are paying the empty rates and the mortgage. If I'm not looking to refinance the investment, and a previous tenant has left, then sometimes I'm willing to sign up a new tenant on a lease of only three years. To cut down on wasted time, you can ask your solicitor to draft the lease up, and you can meet the tenant, sign them up there and then and hand over the keys, going home with the first quarter's rent in hand. I tend to only do this with tenants in lock-up type shops who are unlikely to commit to more than three years.

Technically speaking, I'm sure there will be a clause in your mortgage with the bank that says you need to get their permission to sign the lease to allow a new tenant in your premises. I leave it up to you whether you inform them, especially if it's not particularly good news and the rent you're receiving is less than that of the previous tenant. But for the sake of clarity, I always inform my banks of any change in circumstance!

Another piece of advice to ensure you get your property let as quickly as possible; as soon as your property is vacant, get your solicitor to draw up a draft lease so you are prepared for when you find a potential tenant. This saves you time, and in turn money. Ensure you supply your solicitor with a floor plan to scale of the area you are letting and make it easy as possible to let the building as fast as possible.

I hope you can see from this chapter that I believe in being as flexible as possible to get your vacant property let as soon as possible, and in the best way. When it comes to taking less rent than you feel the property is worth, you need to weigh the situation up for yourself. You may recall in Chapter 3 that I have been on the other side of the landlord-tenant relationship, as the tenant of an office in Norwich. The landlord was too stubborn to consider accepting the same rent I had been paying, which left themwith a vacant property a year later. You don't want to end up in that landlord's situation, holding out for a higher rent that hasn't arrived.

CHAPTER 18

PRE-LETS

The ultimate property deal is when you have sold on the property before you have even actually bought it. You exchange contracts to sell it, as you exchange contracts to purchase the property. Technically, you don't even pay any money because you use the money coming from the purchaser to pay the person selling it to you, as both transactions happen simultaneously.

I have been doing this type of the deal throughout my career. They're difficult to pull off and only work if I am genuinely committed to purchasing the property anyway. If you don't have any interest in retaining it, it doesn't work for me. If there is enough of a margin in it to make it work for me, then there is enough there to make it work for someone who is willing to pay more for it than I am.

This kind of deal is also possible when it comes to letting a commercial space. If you have a good relationship with the local commercial agent, they should have a list of potential tenants that are interesting in renting a building of that size and at the level which you are purchasing.

I find most potential tenants to be genuine and reliable. If you can agree lease terms then they normally proceed and complete the transaction. They are certainly far more reliable than the average residential purchaser.

Many of the major retailers and restaurants have an acquisition list on their website that say where and what kind of premises they are looking to acquire. They will pay a fee to anyone who can introduce them to a building that they eventually rent. So, even if you don't have a premises that might suit them, you might know someone who does and potentially receive an introduction fee if the transaction completes.

Nearly all major tenants will want to sign an agreement to lease prior to the formal lease being signed. This may be because works need to be undertaken prior to the commencement of the lease. This is quite normal, and in my experience, you would be very unlucky if one of these agreements is signed and they decide not to complete on the lease.

It is also possible, that you could find a freehold property that suits them which is vacant, and you are able to purchase it. On the same day you exchange contracts, they sign the agreement to lease. Then, any required works are carried out, at which point the tenant signs the formal lease; the perfect deal!

This means…

- No empty rates

- Rent coming in immediately

- Immediate uplift in value

- Opportunity to refinance and get back the majority of the cash that you put into the transaction back

- Sell the property on to an investor for a profit!

Throughout this book I talk about having options, and the more options you have when purchasing property, the better.

The big new-build commercial developers rarely even purchase land to develop without having a pre-let signed on the development they intend to build.

If a major housebuilder told their estate agent or sales team that they needed to sell the houses and won't even purchase the land until every buyer has exchanged contracts, they would be baffled, but this is exactly what happens with new-build commercial sites.

I find it quite remarkable how these hugely successful commercial developers can pull together these sites in a way that means they don't commit to any serious funding until all the components are in place.

To become a commercial developer in the UK you need a great ability for foresight and getting the right contracts in place. You need to find a land deal subject to planning permission where the major tenants want to trade from. The land is then purchased subject to planning permission. I don't know any commercial developers who would take a chance such a development without obtaining planning permission first and finding a tenant who wishes to take the unit.

This may all sound like rather a tall order, but this is the only way it happens with these larger new-build commercial schemes.

Regarding funding, these larger developments normally turn to pension funds or 'family-run offices'. The latter are generally run by wealthy families that set up their own offices to invest their money into commercial opportunities. The developer will normally fund the planning permission costs, and the land is then purchased subject to planning being granted. Then, they will instruct commercial agents to market the site to find tenants.

In most cases, the financial institution involved will advance most, if not all, the money required to purchase the land as well as the costs to build the development. This is because there is a massive uplift once planning has been granted, and the tenants have signed up to rent the units when completed. Once the investment is complete, they then may well buy the finished investment from the developer. Alternatively, the developer may refinance and retrain this investment; a great business model if you are successful at finding the right sites in the first place, and the right tenants.

And that is basically how the large commercial developments get built, including the large supermarkets, McDonald's, KFC, Costa and the like. One of the exceptions might be something like a new shopping centre where an 'anchor tenant' will be signed up initially. The anchor tenant will be a blue-chip covenant and take up a large space in the new centre, the idea being that because they have committed, this will attract further interest from smaller retailers who may have a similar customer profile. Then, there will be other tenants who wish to be there because of the other names that have signed up. These days, even with the anchor tenant in place, most developers are unlikely to proceed with the development without 50% of the space being pre-let.

I am currently negotiating the purchase of the upper floors of a shopping centre, to be converted into 30 residential apartments. When I went to view it, I met the shopping centre manager who explained that a third of the shops are vacant, and another third are paying 'soft rent'; otherwise known as not the full rent on their lease. The upper floors have never been occupied, and only have a shell finish.

As a commercial developer, I have dreamed of owning a large modern shopping centre like that but as I've never achieved it, perhaps it wasn't such a good idea! As the saying goes, 'all that glitters is not gold'.

CHAPTER 19
FINDING COMMERCIAL DEALS

How to find good property deals is often the reason why people come to my seminar, and is one of the most common questions I am asked. You could even argue that my 40-year career in property has been driven by finding and executing these illusive 'good deals!'

How easy it is to find lucrative deals is dependent on where we are in the property cycle. Historically, we have seen a property recession, on average, every 18 years, and this can make it tough to find the kind of deals we are after.

Recessions present unique opportunities and challenges, but I can confidently say I've made more money on commercial and part-commercial investments when we are coming out of a property recession than at any other time.

COMMERCIAL AGENTS

So how do we go about finding these great deals? The most obvious answer is, of course, through commercial agents. Overall, agents are experienced and professional people with a huge range of contacts in many sectors of the commercial market. These can be broken down into two different groups.

Firstly, there are the large commercial agencies based in in all of the major UK cities. They tend to advise large clients that are looking to let office, retail, or warehouse spaces, or those looking to dispose of commercial buildings throughout the country through private treaty sales. Secondly, you have the local commercial agents. These people tend to be extremely well-connected with many of the investors that operate in their area, as well as potential tenants that are looking to trade locally. They offer your best chance of buying commercial property at the right level and are the best advisors on what rent you can hope to achieve in their area.

If I'm purchasing from one of the large commercial agents, I never ask them to advise me on rent levels. Instead, I always ask the local commercial agents because they have an ear on the ground and are more sensitive to when the local letting markets are improving or getting more challenging. They can come up with the recent rentals as evidence for what you should be able to achieve.

If you are fortunate enough to be one of the larger commercial players, and have large buildings to let, such as retail warehouses, then the national agents are more suited to advise you and find you a tenant. Ultimately, it's horses for courses.

Many of the large agencies get approached by retailers who want to roll out nationally. They are retained by these companies, and then go out to the smaller commercial agents to see what they have in the right areas.

If any of these national agents have smaller commercial units to sell, then sometimes there is an opportunity to buy them below market value because their clients tend to be looking for larger units. It may sound somewhat uncharitable, but the larger agents tend to have limited interest in dealing with a modest shop in a small market town, and this means you may well be able to find yourself a bargain. Then, once purchased, you can put your newly acquired commercial property unit with a local commercial agent, who is likely to do a much better job at reselling or letting it, because they have local knowledge and are more motivated to do so.

It used to be that the Estates Gazette was the property bible for ambitious investors. It would arrive on my doormat on a Saturday morning, and I would spend the weekend making a note of what adverts to follow up on first thing on Monday morning when the agents opened. However, times have really changed, and now it's all about trawling through the websites of commercial agents, most of whom don't do a great job of marketing. I should say that the Estates Gazette is still going, and there is an online version, EG Propertylink.

For the most part, I find that residential estate agents do a much better job of marketing property than their commercial counterparts. Their websites tend to be much better, and up-to-date. They are also fortunate to be able to rely on the major residential portals, Rightmove, Zoopla, etc. Many of the residential portals try to market commercial property, but not very successfully.

Furthermore, there are some residential agents that have a go at selling commercial property, but they tend not to do a very good job. This means you may be able to pick up a bargain from a residential agent attempting to sell a commercial property with little knowledge of that market.

On another note, about the poor marketing that is often carried out by commercial agents, usually clients are charged up front for all advertising and marketing campaigns. Most commercial agents are reluctant to pay upfront cost on top of the commission due from the sale or letting, so don't be confused if you encounter this on your first foray into commercial sales. My advice, if you are committed to selling or letting your property, then you don't have much choice with regards to taking the commercial agent's advice on marketing and paying the up-front fees.

One of the best ways I have found to purchase over the years has been to instruct a commercial agent and retain them to find deals for me, paying a 2% finder's fee upon completion of the transaction. You would be amazed how few people are willing to pay an agent a finder's fee. I cannot stress enough the importance of having a good relationship with a commercial agent that is knowledgeable in the area of your preference. By being willing to pay them a finder's fee, you make sure they are the first person they call when they hear a property that suits you.

BUSINESS TRANSFER AGENTS

One less utilised way of finding commercial deals is to look at what a business transfer agent has for sale. These agents sell businesses, and some have freehold premises. In my experience, most of these businesses start off with very high expectations about how much they expect to sell them for. However, stick at it. Normally they need to sell these businesses, so eventually they are likely to drop to a realistic or even an undervalued business.

Whilst I'm not suggesting that you purchase a trading business, I know I wouldn't want to, there is often opportunities to do a leaseback with them. A leaseback means that you buy the freehold asset, they retain the business, and they rent the premises back from you, or they sell the business with the leasehold going forward. Being a leasehold, their business is now valued at a lower price, and could appeal to more people, potentially giving them a better chance of selling.

In some cases, the business may be worth a negligible amount, and so you can buy it and close it down, or have the current owners do it and then purchase the property vacant.

When you view properties like these, I recommend trying to find out how much they owe the bank, if possible. Knowing this, alongside their reason for selling the business, will give you an indicator of what they can afford to sell the business for. Perhaps they want to retire, or maybe they want to move onto a new venture, bear all of this in mind when you consider your offer. In some cases, it may not be more than what they owe the bank, in this case, be patient. You can probably buy it off the bank in the future.

One negotiating tactic I have used before when buying a business through a business transfer agent, is to pay their commission on behalf of the seller. This type of agent charges quite high rates of commission, compared to a residential or commercial estate agent. And sometimes, the reason the sale cannot proceed is because the seller can't afford the agent's commission, this is when you know they're in serious trouble!

Another reason you may have the opportunity to buy a property from a business transfer agent is because sometimes these owners don't want their business marketed far and wide. These owners are often concerned that their overall trading could be affected, should their customers hear of a potential sale. Generally, my view is that if you want something sold, you want as many people to know about it as possible. Often, I have been able to buy property cheaply because there wasn't much competition, as the property has been poorly marketed and people didn't even realise it was for sale.

AUCTION

I have already mentioned buying at auction. It's a great way of finding profitable deals, many of which have already been with a commercial agent and not sold for one reason or another. It's always a good idea, if you can, to find out the history of the building and understand why it's ended up in the auction. You can contact the original agent that had it for sale and build a relationship with them. Even if you're not successful in that deal, you've then made a good contact for the future and you're now on their radar.

OTHER PROPERTY INVESTORS

Sometimes, opportunities arise when a much larger property investor, who has purchased a portfolio of commercial properties, wants to trade some of those on quickly to reduce borrowings on the whole scheme. I have often managed to do this and work with some large companies.

Normally, I get a phone call from them, saying they have just bought a portfolio, and they are enquiring if I am interested in any of it. And, whilst I appreciate that these contacts take years to cultivate, the sooner you start networking and getting to know these companies, the sooner you can get the "crumbs from the rich man's table."

What many people don't realise is that these companies are often buying very large portfolios at huge discounts, and so they can then pass on some of these discounts to the rest of us. You want them to know who you are, and that you buy what you say you're going to buy, and that you get on and do it quickly. Operating in this way gets you a reputation for being straightforward and assists in building these contacts that little bit quicker.

It's so important to have as many contacts as possible, and for the contacts you do have to trust you and know you keep your word, whilst also being flexible enough to get deals done. This applies to everyone, from the commercial agent, to the auctioneer, to other investors.

CHAPTER 20
TRADING LEASEHOLD & FREEHOLD PROPERTY

In the previous chapter, we discussed finding good property deals, and one of the ways you can do this is through traders and investors, who perhaps want to sell either part of a property, or part of a portfolio.

Let me give an example:

I'm currently in the process of buying large building, the upper floors are currently offices but can be converted to residential under permitted development. The ground floor must remain as commercial. I'm paying £750,000 for it freehold. So, having agreed to purchase the building, I immediately get in touch with agents I know to see if they have anyone who might be interested to buy the upper floors for £550,000. As it happens, they have two people who might be interested. Getting in touch with them means that I might have done a great deal here, and if not, I've made two new property contacts who might purchase deals from me in the future.

Then, I speak to a commercial agent I know, and ask if there are any tenants looking for the commercial unit on the ground floor. I stress that I am happy to split it into smaller units if needed. The commercial agent comes back to me with three potential tenants: a gym, a tenpin bowling alley, and a Christian organisation.

As an aside, it's interesting how many small churches are springing up all over the place and are taking on commercial buildings that were previously retail. I recently spoke at an event in Kensington. I walked into the room that I thought the event was being held in. I was greeted very warmly, more so than usual, and found the warm welcome a bit strange. It wasn't until the Pastor, a fellow property investor who recognised me and introduced himself, explained that this is a church gathering and my meeting was in the next room. The first time I ever heard of a hotel meeting room being used for a church service!

So, as you have probably gathered, before I have even purchased a building, I'm considering all the different ways that I can find a tenant, and even how I might be able to sell of uppers, either subject to planning or as they are. Another strategy I sometimes employ when buying a part-let investment is to immediately sell off the occupied parts, either at auction or to a fellow investor I know who may be interested. Both of these strategies will reduce your interest costs and allow you to get some cash out of the deal quicker to fund your next purchase.

Very few commercial property investors like to purchase on a long leasehold. Most investors wish to purchase freehold, even if they are just taking the ground floor, they will then usually grant a long lease to whoever is taking the upper floors. This is called title splitting, when you split an existing land title into smaller pieces or create leaseholds within the building. This is all dealt with by your solicitor and is quite a simple process. Please don't listen to these so-called property educators that will make out it's something new and exciting: property developers have been doing this forever!

Hopefully, this gives you a good example of what is possible if you purchase the property for the right amount of money. They say that "the selling is in the buying" and I believe that this is true.

Now, frustratingly for the moment, there is no conclusion to this deal but I'm sure you'll hear about it in the future if you continue to follow me.

The above example is just one of many types of deal that I've done over my career, as have many other property traders. It may be that you wish to use auctions to trade and not only just to purchase investment stock, but also to sell. Auctions are a great way of selling and trading your investments, and an advantage is that once the hammer comes down the proceeds will normally be in your account within 28 days. Selling at auction is great for cash flow and there's no one asking you hundreds of questions through your solicitors and taking up to six months to exchange contracts!

When I buy a property, I like as many options as possible out of a deal. The more options you have the better, you want to have the ability to remain flexible in a deal.

Remember, if you're selling or purchasing a leasehold commercial property, then you will need to adjust the yield by one or two percent, as it will be valued at slightly less than if the investment were freehold.

As I mentioned before, many investors just won't even consider a property that is not freehold. This gives me even more opportunity to purchase an investment at a discount. If a property is on a 999-year lease with zero ground rent, then I consider it as good as freehold. However, if a property is on a 125-year lease and 50 years have passed since it started, then you certainly have to take more of a view as to the discount compared to a freehold yield.

As the leasehold years go down, so does the value, and in turn the yield rises. In theory, if the lease were to run down to zero, then the property would be returned to the freeholder for nothing. This never happens because there is always a deal to be done with the freeholder at some point to extend the lease. And once you've extended the lease back to its original length, you can then trade the building on again. A longer lease will make it more mortgageable and, therefore, more attractive to another investor at a lower yield.

If you plan to buy an investment that is leasehold, my advice is to try and buy the freehold from the current freeholder at some point. Depending on the length of the lease, it may be relatively cheap to purchase, and then your investment will become freehold. If you can get the deal done for a good price, then you can easily trade the property on for a profit.

Sometimes, these long leasehold investments are described as a head lease. A lease that is granted by the tenant to a sub-tenant for a shorter period is sometimes called an under lease.

CHAPTER 21
CONVERTING COMMERCIAL TO RESIDENTIAL

I haven't forgotten that this is a book about commercial property, but I want you to have all the information you could need in your armoury. There is always a possibility that you buy a commercial investment, it becomes vacant and you struggle to find the right tenant.

Whatever the situation, it's always best to check out all of your options. One of them could be to convert some or all of the building to residential, either as flats or vertical splits to create townhouses. Any form of conversion requires full building regulation approval. For conversion costs, you should speak to a quantity surveyor, as they will give you a good indication as to what people are working in terms of $£/ft^2$, as these figures change over time.

When I say "depending on specification" I mean, if you're converting a luxurious property in Hampstead, you can expect to spend more than in an area where property values are lower. This is all to do with the overall quality of finishes that are required, for example, better kitchens and bathrooms. Not only does this make the units saleable when compared to others nearby, it also increases value. Whereas in a cheaper residential area, spending the extra money is unlikely to be so profitable in terms of sale price.

If you are undertaking any building work, whether commercial or residential, it is essential that you have a Schedule of Works prepared by a building surveyor. Surveyors are indispensable to any development project. The schedule will include all works that are required as per planning permission and the building regulation approval that must be sought. That is, unless it is under permitted development, and even then, all building regulations need to be applied for and approved.

Following your building surveyor completing the schedule of works, it then goes to the builders to tender, with each builder tendering on the same basis. Once the tenders are back, the surveyor will then offer their advice on who you should chose and how long you can expect the work to take.

When choosing a builder, I don't always go for the cheapest tender. I like to know what other work they have done recently and talk to their former clients: did they come in on time and on budget? This is very important. I have bought and developed over 4000 properties and employed great building surveyors throughout to oversee construction, and I can count the number of times I have had a completely smooth construction period without delays and within budget on one hand. So, whilst you can't guarantee anything with construction, you can give yourself the best possible chances.

It's interesting to note that the smoothest development I have ever done was when I spent £26 million on 150 flats which were left partly finished by a developer that went bankrupt. It came in on time and on budget. At this level, the contractors are as much a management company as anything else. These large companies employ no tradesmen whatsoever anymore, but rather manage the contractors. This system with huge management and using top subcontractors is the answer for large developments, but just isn't practical and would be far too costly on smaller projects.

Having chosen your builder, the surveyor will then prepare a JCT (Joint Contracts Tribunal) small works contract: a fixed-price contract with penalties for late completion, paid by the builder. In my experience, every builder will find an excuse as to why they weren't on time, and signing up to that is more a gesture of intention and good faith rather than actually receiving compensation. However, of course if your chosen builder isn't keeping up with the program of work as outlined by your surveyor and doesn't have reasonable reasons, for example weather conditions or availability of materials, then they need to be paying penalties for late completion.

I always do my best with builders to keep a good working relationship and ensure that the development is carried out in a professional and friendly manner. I also ensure that this is kept up should any issues arise. I hope that the builder does the same.

If you are converting above a ground floor where there is still a tenant trading, this can cause big problems when it comes to getting certain works. This is a particular challenge with regards to anything that affects the floors, soundproofing, or getting access to the ground floor for access to waste pipes or electrical supplies. Before you start work, you must read their lease to see whether it allows for maintenance or renewals. Realistically, access can only be given when the business is closed at night or over weekends, with everything being returned to good order before trading can start on the next working day.

Even if it costs more money to raise the floors at the first-floor level, so you can put soundproofing, fireproofing and other services in, it's essential that you do so, as these are then completely under your ownership and control. This will save you time and trouble in the future if there is enough ceiling height. You need to check that you have at least 7 ft of headroom once the floor has been raised and after all works are completed.

A few years ago, I purchased a building let to Iceland, the frozen food retailer, with vacant upper floors. In the lease there was no allowance for the freeholder to gain access to do works from their shop. I began negotiating with head office to see whether we could undertake work at the weekends and evenings but had no success. Furthermore, if I had raised the floor, I wouldn't have had the head height required to pass building regulations.

Consider my experience here a learning curve of your own. If you are looking to purchase a building with planning or potential planning for apartments above the ground floor, you need to make sure you can undertake the works to get this done.

Having obtained planning, I managed to sell the building off at a profit, presumably to someone who didn't look closely enough at the details to realise this would be a very challenging development. Make sure that's not you!

When the works have been completed, the council will issue the completion certificate, allowing occupancy of the premises or put it on the market to be sold. If you're looking to sell the flats, these should be sold on a 990-year lease at zero ground rent.

If selling, you need to prepare a budget forecast for what the service charges are likely to be on an annual basis, a specialist property management company will be able to do this for you. Service charges should include insurance, cleaning of common areas, management fees, and a sinking fund. The sinking fund allows money to be held by a management company which is used to carry out future works to the building.

If you are looking to sell the flats on, you also need a ten-year building warranty. Until recently this was only required on new-build properties, but now most lending institutions require this for conversions too. On a small development you can expect this to cost around £2,000 per unit, on a larger development there is usually a discount for volume. If it's a new build, then it's likely to be cheaper still. You are far better off to get this sorted out straight away as getting a warranty retrospectively is far more expensive. A warranty will involve a monthly inspection to ensure that the works taking place are of a good standard, allowing them to grant you the certificate upon completion of the work.

You should be aware that when converting above commercial property, they will be more difficult to sell than a purely residential development, as some lending institutions will not lend directly above commercial, and those that will charge more interest to the borrower. It's also important that you consider the type of commercial premises. For instance, I would be unlikely to want to invest large sums of money converting to residential above a restaurant or a pub; very few people over the age of 21 would want to live above a pub! Even more difficult are those above take-away restaurants; these are almost impossible to sell and challenging to rent. In that situation, the best tenants are the people who work below.

If you are looking to retain and rent then you are under less pressure to repay the bank, and hopefully can refinance once the flats are completed and let. You will want to refinance because you are likely on a development loan basis, which is more expensive than a long-term loan. If you are looking to retain and rent the flats, don't be tempted to shortcut on construction, you still need your certificate from the council and the building regulations are just the same.

You may decide that you want to sell half and keep half of the units, which is, in my opinion, a great strategy.

And finally, when you're developing a flat, do not expect to get the same for your flat above a commerical property as one that is not. When you're looking on Rightmove, don't compare a two bedroom flat in a residential area to yours of the same size and standard above a commercial premises; it won't be worth quite as much.

CHAPTER 22
BUILDING COMMERCIAL UNITS

Building new commercial units is not for every commercial investor. However, for some, particularly those who are builders by trade and want to get into commercial property, this could be the right progression for their investment portfolio, as long as you obtain a pre-let.

Very few of the large commercial developers ever build 'on spec'. Meaning, they don't build commercial units without having a tenant already signed up to move into the property once completed.

The Government is very keen on the redevelopment of brownfield sites. Brownfield sites are those that were formerly designated for another use; perhaps there was a redundant factory on the site or other commercial buildings that are in extremely poor condition. Therefore, demolition and redevelopment of the site becomes the most attractive and financially viable proposition.

Currently, the Government is guaranteeing planning permission on any site that has currently been used for another purpose. I would expect local authorities to be cooperative, especially if it will create employment, a key factor in why local authorities are concerned about losing commercial space to residential.

As well as demolition costs, there are two more things you must be aware of. The first is ground contamination. You will need to have a test carried out to confirm that the soil is not contaminated and that you don't need to pile the site. This is when, instead of traditional foundations, a piling rig is brought in and drives precast concrete piles into the ground, sometimes up to a depth of 25 metres, because the land you intend to build on is unstable. This will increase development costs.

The second, in town and city centre locations, is an archaeological dig. If local authorities believe their could be some historical importance attached to the site, your development will be held up for around six to nine months as part of the planning conditions prior to commencement of the works.

For many, warehouse opportunities are of greater interest. They are simple to construct, and cheap in comparison to building a shop with flats above. Moreover, you might be able to get some pre-lets, or if you're building ten units you could phase the development; do the first five, get those let and move onto the next five after refinancing.

Furthermore, businesses that are interested in these warehouse units are more likely to buy them freehold. Many small companies have a self-administered pension that directors pay money into on a regular basis. Funds in pensions are sometimes used to purchase commercial property, then the business rents the units back from the pension fund.

A good thing about new-build commercial units, is that until they are fitted out, if they have been left with a shell finish with no facilities inside like kitchens and toilets, they are not habitable; meaning that there are no rates payable until you have a tenant who fits it out ready for occupation.

One of the challenges presented by new builds is their lack of fit-out, and many tenants are not prepared to take on a shell finished building. To fit out a unit requires financial resources, I'm talking about plastering the walls, putting in the electrics, suspended ceilings, and so on. Therefore, it's down to you as a landlord to complete the works if you want your property let. However, I recommend getting a contribution from the tenants for these works, depending on the length of lease they are signing. When it comes to budgeting your construction costs, I would always allow for the full fit-out just in case. In terms of yield, a new build will attract a better valuation compared to a property that is older and will need more maintenance soon.

Whatever new-build commercial you plan to do, most local authorities are likely to be enthusiastic about your plans. As mentioned before, they are constantly concerned about lack of employment in the local area, particularly with more commercial properties becoming residential under the Government's current permitted development rules. And if I were very cynical, I could also say that they get much higher rates from commercial premises than residential.

CHAPTER 23
MULTI-LET INVESTMENT

Many people think that multi-lets are the perfect commercial investment. Even the banks are comfortable with mixed-use investments and, in many cases, will lend a higher loan to value ratio than for single let investments. The reason for this is that you are "hedging your bets," there's safety in numbers.

My thoughts on this type of popular investment are you need to be careful. The commercial agent will hype it up saying what a safe investment it is with the flexibility of many different tenants and rental income streams. I believe that some of these investments go for very inflated prices because investors think that the more tenants, the safer the investment. However, in my view - depending on the mix at, let's say, ten units - is that the more tenants in the building, the more chance there is that some cannot, or will not pay and do a runner.

I'm not convinced that this type of investment is a safer bet than having one very good tenant held on a longer lease. I understand the reasons why some think it is better because, of course, you've always got some money coming in rather than potentially none if the one tenant goes bankrupt or leaves at the end of the lease.

However, if you buy a multi-let investment at say 9% yield and there are four tenants, it only requires one of those to leave and suddenly you have an investment with a yield of 7% or less, depending on which tenant vacates.

This is especially important if you are in the process of purchasing the investment. Far be it from me to say that someone may be misleading a purchaser if they don't declare that they knew a tenant was shortly about to leave the property, but this does make a difference to the value you should be paying for it, unless, of course, they can replace the tenant prior to completion. I would offer less money unless it's sold as described. If the current owner wishes to pay the rent for the vacant unit until it is let, then that might be an acceptable compromise. They are very likely to ask for a backstop for, say, 12 months, but at least that gives you the opportunity to find the right tenant.

Because the building is split into several units, the leases are more likely to be on shorter internal and repairing leases. They may well be businesses that are just starting up and are soon going to do one of two things: either not make it and end up giving up the lease, or make a real success of their business and require a bigger premises and leave on that basis.

The mix of tenants can be a problem too. For instance, you could have a tenant with a business that is quite noisy and have other tenants in the building who are not happy, constantly complaining about the noise created. They may all share a kitchen, which can cause problems. Parking can be another issue when there aren't enough spaces, so the tenants are continually fighting about who gets which space, depending on when they arrive in the mornings. If these problems persist there's only one outcome which is that they will leave, and you will be left with one problematic tenant!

In recent years we have seen a real rise in the number of people working from home, and these are the type of investments that can suffer. There may be only one or two employees per lease in the property in the first place, so you could find tenants making the decision to go completely remote.

Now all the above may sound very negative and I don't mean it to be so, but I'm just purely pointing out that perhaps the multi-let investment is not quite as good as people think it is. I'm not advising against the purchase of these types of investments, I'm just advising against being sucked into paying a very low yield to do so, because some of that rent that you're buying may ultimately be short-term and I expect, on relatively short leases. I would not be looking to buy a mixed-use investment at under 10% and probably nearer 10 to 15%, depending on the length of leases the tenants are on.

CHAPTER 24
RENTING TO LARGE ORGANISATIONS

To anyone reading this book who is renting, or likely renting to a large organisation soon, I say congratulations. Whether they are blue chip covenants or companies that are rolling out a programme of expansion across the UK, these are the ultimate tenants for any landlord to have.

In my experience, although financially powerful, larger tenants are far easier to deal with than smaller local or regional ones. One of the reasons is that large organisations usually appoint a national commercial agent to act on their behalf, who then contacts a local agent to see what accommodation is available to suit their requirements. With organisations on this scale, you are unlikely to be dealing with the owner of the business and they're far less likely to quibble over the small details, and the odd thousand pounds here or there won't make much difference to their bottom line.

If your prospective tenant is on a mission to expand, they will have a target of several stores they need to open within a specific time frame to keep their investors happy, and this is worth remembering during negotiations. Agents acting on their behalf will generally be as flexible as they can be and are motivated to get the job done because they earn a commission on the completion of each lease, much like your agent.

Another bonus when dealing with companies of this size is that they are nearly always willing to invest money into your building, sometimes in very large amounts. They use very expensive and very skilled shopfitters that work quickly as soon as the lease is signed, so that they can get trading as fast as possible. Each store will follow the same fit-out design and it will be of good quality.

When negotiating with this type of tenant, you need to get the full schedule of works that they intend to carry out, that way you can intervene early if there's anything that doesn't meet your approval or that might interfere with any neighbouring tenants.

All of this sounds wonderful, right? I know the tenant will sign a long lease. Then, they will spend potentially hundreds of thousands on your building, increasing the value of your investment. What's the catch? Some of these companies will ask for a contribution towards the fit out, that's the one you thought they were paying for. This could be as much as three years' rent, and sometimes even more, depending on the length of lease they are willing to sign. I'm told by many commercial agents that tenants are getting increasingly greedy with the inclusion of this capon (Chapter 27), as they feel that landlords are under more pressure to get their space let. Moreover, they sometimes expect this money paid on signing of the lease, causing landlords significant cash flow problems. So, while on the face of it these tenants seem ideal, they can on occasion come with conditions attached. These companies really have the upper hand when it comes to negotiations.

However, most landlords can find the money to pay the capon because of the increased value of their investment, and the companies know this. It's therefore a case of organising the refinance on the back of an improved valuation, subject to the tenant signing the lease.

Overall, I am still happy to deal with these types of tenants given the increase in value they add to your portfolio. As landlords, we must accept that this is how the business is now, and we would all rather have the tenant than not.

CHAPTER 25

THE CHALLENGES OF BEING A COMMERCIAL LANDLORD

I hope I haven't deterred any commercial landlords among the readers. I have tried to be honest, pointing out the benefits while also making you aware of the challenges in the industry. I now want to take this one step further and share with you what can happen when things go very wrong.

The term 'underwater' is one that you sadly hear too often among investors. It describes what happens when the following scenario unfolds.

A landlord has owned an investment property for the last three years, during which period they have received £100,000 rent per annum. However, the lease is up for review and the tenant does not want to renew or has gone into receivership. Because the property has been let at £100,000 a year and was valued at an 8% yield making it worth £1.25 million. Rather than sell it for that, the landlord decides to retain it as a long-term investment. Having had the property revalued, they remortgaged and took out a £700,000 loan, enabling them to buy more property.

The advantage of not selling but refinancing is that you do not pay tax on the money raised on a remortgage. It surprises me that the treasury hasn't yet taken hold of this; taxing people as if the property had been sold would raise millions of pounds for the government.

A year later and the property is still without a tenant. The bank then decides to have the property revalued and with no tenant they decide it is valued at £400,000. Not only that, but in the valuer's opinion and in the current market, the rental value is now £50,000. The bank reports the findings to the landlord and, at the same time asks them to either put in additional funds to rebalance the banking mandate of loan to value or increase the personal guarantee that was set up when he originally took out the loan. Such guarantees must be accompanied by a statement of assets, meaning an affidavit confirming the worth of your current net assets. In this situation, there is no ideal outcome.

Even the investors who can find a large sum of money to put back into a building to reduce debt are extremely reluctant to do so. A personal guarantee is less painful in principle, but very stressful for the entire family. If the landlord has crystallised a loss by selling the property, at this point the bank will ask for the personal guarantee to be honoured. The landlord can negotiate payment over a period, but the bank will likely charge interest. Many people in this situation would need to sell assets to raise the money, and the money made from this is likely taxable.

The chances of the property being let over and above the rental value given by the bank's valuer are remote. However, it's worth trying to find a tenant at a higher rent than advised, this will buy the landlord some time with the bank.

Most banks don't work very quickly, but eventually, the landlord is likely to be referred to the recovery department at their bank.

Eventually, the bank will lose patience with the landlord trying to get the premises let and will call in the loan on the property.

The bank has been quite clever here in asking for further security on the loan, but ultimately, the action they will take is really the same as if the landlord had not committed to further funds or personal guarantees.

The lesson I am attempting to convey here is that whatever action you choose to take in this scenario will only delay the inevitable. I know people who wish they hadn't put in the extra money the bank had asked for, and I also know some who wish they hadn't signed a further guarantee to stave off the inevitable. It's a difficult decision, and sometimes hard to see the wood for the trees when you're under that sort of pressure. This is what is happening to landlords right now throughout the UK, and in my opinion, will continue to happen, as properties come to the end of their lease and the tenant does not wish to renew.

Please be very careful when looking to buy properties that are let on relatively short leases. It's especially tempting to think that they will sign a new lease when the existing one runs out when they are a household name. I've already written about my personal experiences on this earlier in the book, so please calculate that rent may be halved at the end of the lease, especially if it's in a town centre location. If it sounds too good to be true, most of the time it is.

CHAPTER 26

WHERE TO BUY YOUR INVESTMENT

At the start of the year, I am normally asked by the media what I think will happen in the residential market over the coming 12 months. I generally film something on a similar theme for my YouTube channel as well. At the end of last year, I was the guest speaker at a property club, and my answer was, "there are only three things that can happen: the market can stay the same, the market can go up, or it can go down." I appreciate that this isn't very helpful, but I do go on to make an educated guess as to what I expect to see. Ultimately, predicting the market is a fool's game, and all you can do is use experienced gained from the past.

The same is true when we look at the market on a micro scale and are considering where to buy your investment. You can take advice from many expert reviews, draw on their years of experience, but there are many aspects to consider, particularly on your first investment property.

Hopefully, you won't be going to the property every month sorting out one problem or another, as the terms of the lease will state that the tenants are responsible for repairs. However, if you purchase locally, within an hour's drive, then if there are issues or problems that you need to get involved with, it's much easier to do than if you're five hours away. Addtionally, you may have local information about the tenant that is going into your premises. Furthermore, you are far more likely to have a good grasp on the local market. And, as we all know, knowledge is power, particularly when it comes to purchasing a long-term investment.

Many years ago, I purchased a derelict commercial building which I thought was going to be right in front of a new shopping centre, if it ever got built. The good news is it was built. The bad news is it faced the other way, and my shops were looking over the rear of the building onto the access for deliveries. It wasn't the uplift in value I had hoped for!

Let us assume you have found a suitable investment property. The building that you wish to purchase will be valued by the bank. They will instruct a chartered surveyor to value it on the bank's behalf, although you will be paying the valuation fee. This valuation should give you some confidence that you are paying the right amount for the property. I will make you aware at this point, that it is quite common, especially on smaller commercial investments, for the property to be down valued by the valuer.

If this happens, there are three potential courses of action.

The first is to approach the current owners, explain that the property has been down valued by the bank, and tell them you are only prepared to pay the amount at which it has been valued.

The second, ignore the advice of the valuer, you might completely disagree with them. If this is the case, I always try to speak to the valuers, and see how they have come to the conclusion they have. After which, you can decide whether they are right or wrong. Either way, it's highly unlikely that the valuer will change their mind unless there has been a major misunderstanding surrounding the leases. At this point, you'll need to put in the extra money required to cover the down valuation, as the bank will not be willing to lend as much as the full purchase price. You could also try meeting the owner in the middle between what they think the building is worth and what the valuer believes; I've used this tactic to negotiate many times.

The third option is to walk away from the deal completely. Sometimes this is the best course of action, although nobody wants to waste the time and money it's taken to get to this point. But, as Donald Trump once said, "Sometimes your best investments are the ones you don't make."

If you do decide to walk away from the deal, you will probably encounter serious pressure from the commercial agent who has sold the investment to you in principle. They will suggest that this type of thing never happens to them, that it's appalling, and you have made a serious mistake. Let me tell you now, they probably have a deal fall through under similar circumstances every month! Be strong, be polite, and stick to your guns on this.

After having their tantrum and speaking to the owner, the agent may come back and ask how much you would pay. At this point, I don't like answering that question, I tend to throw it back to them and ask what reduction the owner would accept. You've now got the owner to agree to a reduction before you've even begun to negotiate the price any further. This is a clever tactic, even if it's not the original plan!

Anyway, this chapter is about where to buy your investment property. These days, you can do an awful lot of research to find out employment and population levels. There are some places in the UK where the population is decreasing; generally, not a good sign but there are exceptions to every rule.

The government can also have a key role in your decision making on this. They introduced freeport status for several coastal areas where ports already exist, some of which have been deprived for many years. This can be a major boost for private companies looking to relocate to these areas to take advantage of the tax-free trade.

There are some areas of the UK where there are specific tax incentives for employers to set up. And, these are well worth looking at, but usually in quite deprived areas of the country.

Years ago, the quickest and best way I found to learn about a particular town or city was to jump in a taxi and have them drive me around. The taxi driver would tell me more in 15 minutes than any estate agent or commercial agent ever would and with far more honesty; for example, which areas the police won't go into at night and so on. The internet is a cheaper and more convenient way of doing the same job. The crime figures in the area are a very useful guide, as well as seeing what shops are trading in areas that you're interested in investing in.

Sometimes, the local political scene is also a good indicator of what might happen. For example, some areas have been Labour for many years and have a feel of deprivation and negativity to them, Or, some have recently voted in a Conservative MP, and interestingly are one of the beneficiaries of the £25 million Town Fund. Another example, if an MP has a slim majority, they will get as much support as the party can give to help them win at the next election, including funding from central government, perhaps to improve the road layout or the local hospital.

So, when it really comes down to it, where you invest is all about personal preference. I hope that the information given here has provided you with to consider when making your decision and planning out your strategy.

CHAPTER 27

GLOSSARY OF TERMS AND EXAMPLES

PREMIUMS

A premium is a payment made to the landlord by a tenant to enter a lease. These days, this happens very rarely, but perhaps you've had a tenant leave a building with rent owing. In that case, you may have accepted the contents as part payment of the outstanding rent. In the past, I have managed to receive premiums from the ingoing tenant. On one occasion, it was when I was renting out a restaurant and on another, a takeaway business. I always consider this a real bonus because I would have let to the tenant on both occasions anyway, without the premium. It's always important to be on your toes and quick-witted when you meet the tenant. I like to do this, if at all possible, to see how keen they are to move in, to judge for myself whether I think I'm going to get my rent and if there is a chance, they might offer a premium. In both the above examples, fortunately, they did. It might have been the fact that I mentioned I had interest from other parties. Who knows!

REVERSE PREMIUMS

A reverse premium is a capital sum paid by the landlord or outgoing tenant to induce a new tenant to enter into a leasehold agreement.

This can be a very lucrative outcome if you have an alternative use for the property. Many of the larger tenants look to downsize their operations and, as such, some will look to try and get out of their current leases. Some tenants may have signed up to leases that still have years left to run. The longer the lease must run, potentially, the more money you can get out of them to be released from their commitment. This is a reverse premium.

A friend of mine got close to £1 million out of a very well-known pub chain that wanted to get out of a lease that was £180,000 per annum. The lease had more than ten years to run. He paid for dinner that night!

LEASEBACK

A leaseback is where the owner of a commercial property wishes to remain in occupation but sells the freehold. They then enter into a lease with the new owner. The leaseback I did at Cambridge United would be a prime example of this.

My only concern with leasebacks is, why is the freehold owner of the property selling? If it's for expansion and they wish to grow the business in other areas of the country, then I see this as a positive move. However, most leasebacks in my experience come about because the freeholder is under financial pressure within the business. They need to raise capital in order for it to carry on. If that is the case, they are just delaying the inevitable. If they wish to do a leaseback on that basis, then the business will continue to get into further financial trouble in the long term, which ultimately means that you won't have a tenant. If you have an alternative use for the building, all well and good. If not, it can be a disaster.

If you are considering the purchase of a commercial investment where a leaseback has taken place in the past, be very careful. The rent may well have been inflated beyond what it should be for premises of that size, the reason being the original owner needed to raise a certain amount of cash and so the building was sold on an inflated valuation based on what the building was rented back for. This is called a rack rent – see below.

The other issue to be careful of is, if the rent is too high and the tenant cannot sustain the rent payments in the future, then you have no investment at all!

RACK RENT

When the term rack rent is used in the context of an investment property, it means that the property is let for the maximum amount it can be let for. It can also be described as a full rent. When you hear this term, you must be very cautious because, as far as I am concerned, it's a warning that there is no opportunity of any uplift in the rent, potentially for many years, as it's already rented at its maximum level, or well beyond, for the current market.

CAPON

A capon is when a tenant wishes to have a cash incentive to sign a new lease and is normally used by national companies who wish to expand across the UK as a way of paying for their fit-out costs.

However, if you had a particularly tricky property to let you could entice potential tenants by offering a form of reverse capon where you give them a lump sum to take on the lease. This is obviously a dangerous game to play, and one or two potential tenants may try to take advantage of your generous nature! However, if you need a lease signed and you can tie up the tenants in such a way that the money you have given is secured in some way, then in specific circumstances, it may be a possible solution and get you out of a challenging situation.

RENT KICKBACK

A rent kickback is probably more commonly used by landlords than the reverse capon. In my case, I offer to give the tenant some of the rent back on a quarterly basis in order to incentivise them to sign the lease on the terms I initially want.

So, for instance, if I want £30,000 per annum and they're only prepared to pay £25,000, then if they pay the full rent on time I will then return the balance, going forward, for as long as the agreement has been negotiated. Of course, if they don't pay on time, they won't receive the kickback. Sometimes, I find this is better than a rent-free period where they pay nothing for a certain length of time. I would always inform the lender that this is the agreement I have reached with the tenant.

RENT-FREE PERIOD

This is the most common incentive given by a landlord to a tenant. As I've already mentioned, make sure that you get some commitment from the tenant in the first place before you start giving away months and months of rent free. I always try to get the first three months' rent out of them, then give them the rent-free period that they have negotiated and then after, they're back to full rent.

DEFERRED RENT PAYMENT

The use of deferred rent payment is very helpful when I have a tenant who is struggling to pay all the rent on a quarterly or monthly basis. Many landlords fall into the trap of letting tenants off the rent completely. By agreeing on a deferred payment, you are not doing so, and the rent is still legally due. This hopefully means that, as the business improves again for them, they will be able to pay over and above the monthly rent to reduce the arrears.

But remember: if you've entered this type of arrangement, you may not be able to gain possession of the building, should you wish to, for non-payment of rent. So, please take advice from your solicitor before you enter into this type of agreement.

ASSIGNMENT OF LEASE

This is when one tenant decides to assign the lease to another tenant, and it normally requires permission from the landlord. Though most leases probably say that permission must not be unreasonably withheld. Grounds for withholding, I suppose, would be if the incoming tenant was a former bankrupt. But even then, if they can prove that they are now solvent, they would be allowed to take over the existing lease. You could try and use the situation to your advantage and ask them whether they would like to sign a lease extension at the same time. Most tenants are initially enthusiastic and optimistic about their chances of being successful in their new premises.

LEASE EXTENSIONS

Most people tend to leave negotiations about extending the lease until near the end of the existing term. I personally think this is far too late in the process and prefer to start the process much sooner. You may wonder why a tenant with a year or two remaining on their current lease would want to negotiate at that point in time, when many may not have decided whether they are remaining in the premises at the end of the lease. Well, firstly by offering them an extension to the lease, you are confirming that you want them to stay, and they can plan their future business strategy with more clarity and confidence. You may be prepared to give them a slight incentive with regards to a change in the length of future rent reviews, possibly even reducing the rent slightly from its current level if they were to sign a lease extension early. You could offer a cash kickback on the signature of the lease extension possibly if a further incentive was required, you may not need to give away anything but if you don't start the negotiations early, you may never know.

DILAPIDATIONS

This is when a tenant is moving out at the end of the lease and there is a clause in the lease that says the property has to be put back to the condition it was in when the lease started.

Here are a couple of points to remember. The first is that you need to have a detailed schedule of condition within the lease or photographic evidence, which is the cheaper alternative, to prove what the condition was in the first place. The second, is that if you're looking to redevelop the property, it's unlikely these days that you will be able to use the dilapidation clause, as if you're doing so anyway, any works that the tenant would do to put the property back to its original condition will be a waste of time. Tenants and their advisors have got wise to this, as have some of the courts.

In terms of the negotiation, normally both parties will appoint a surveyor who is a specialist in dilapidations. The landlord's surveyor will go into the property and assess the condition and how much it will cost to put it right. Then the tenant normally has the option of putting the works right themselves or writing a cheque for the sum that's been calculated by the landlord. Quite often, a cash negotiated payment is the best route to go for the landlord rather than the tenant going through the palaver of refurbishing the premises. Not only that but if you manage to find a tenant to take it in its existing condition, any cash sum you receive from the outgoing tenant is a bonus.

CAPITAL ALLOWANCES

Capital allowances are a means of saving tax when your business buys a capital asset.

This is the latest hot topic among property people, with a number of companies formed recently in order to survey the property and calculate how much you can claim on fixed items such as air-conditioning units, central heating, and the like. There is no cash to be received back, but you get a tax allowance towards your annual net profit. These companies take a percentage of the agreed capital allowance that is accepted by HMRC.

This topic is really for the experts who specialise in it, but I would start off by talking to your accountant, who should have a pretty good grasp of the subject. Currently, many people are trying to claim these tax breaks. I'm not convinced that all of them will be successful.

I'm sure the Treasury did not contemplate that when an investor purchased a property, they would be able to make a successful claim for capital allowances, especially when they are likely to rip out those items installed by a former owner. I expect, in the future, this loophole will be closed down, but for the moment it's worth investigating. When you are in the process of purchasing commercial property, you need to ask the existing owners whether they have claimed the capital allowances or not. If they haven't, then you must get them to confirm through their solicitors so that you're able to make a claim once completion takes place. I wouldn't ask them this question prior to agreeing on the price because they may then stick out for more money if they think you can claim the allowances. It's purely a bonus to the deal rather than a deal-breaker in my view. You should always assume when purchasing that you can't claim capital allowances back until it's confirmed in writing that you can.

PRE-LET

This refers to a situation where a tenant has signed a legal agreement to take a lease out on a building, normally prior to any building work taking place. Please don't assume that just because you have a tenant who says they will take it, but without any legal agreement signed, this is a pre-let. That's just hoping that you have a tenant!

With a pre-let, make sure that there is a schedule as to the condition of the building that the tenant is taking on so that there are no arguments about a particular finish to the interior of the building that was expected and not provided. See chapter 18 for more information on pre-lets.

VAT

I wanted to mention VAT, and to be honest, I didn't know which chapter to put it in so it's here! This can be a very complicated area when purchasing a property. In many cases, the current owner will have an option of whether to charge the buyer VAT on the purchase. There is a form that is filled in, which is the default VAT exemption. The only downside to this for the person selling is that they won't be able to recover VAT on costs associated with the sale.

Properties that have VAT on them are normally much harder to sell as the buyers must find an extra 20%, the chargeable rate at the time of publication, in order to complete the purchase. Of course, it's important, if that is the case, that the company making the purchase becomes VAT registered. In normal circumstances, the

VAT can be reclaimed within 3 months. Please seek advice from VAT experts prior to purchasing a commercial property.

STAMP DUTY

When this book was published, the level of stamp duty on buying commercial property was 4%. Please check what the level is at the time of reading. There are several companies around who allegedly specialise in getting you out of paying any stamp duty or reducing it substantially. I've investigated this in the past and I've had no success whatsoever with these companies when it comes to commercial property.

The situation may be different if a building is inhabitable or derelict. However, most solicitors are very cautious, which is exactly what you want them to be, along with your accountant, so as not to get you into any legal or financial difficulties. Ultimately, it is the solicitor that gets fined if there is a mistake in the amount of stamp duty charged. They are very unlikely to want to take any risk whatsoever and to be quite honest I don't wish to either.

The government website GOV.UK is very comprehensive and has a large section on both stamp duty and VAT and what the rules are.

THE LANDLORD & TENANT ACT 1954 & SECURITY OF TENURE

If a commercial contract falls within the 1954 act, you should be aware that should a premises come to the end of its term, as a landlord you are required to reoffer the tenant a lease on the same terms. This does not mean that you are required to offer it at the same rent. This provision can be 'contracted out' of a lease, so you should discuss this with your solicitor.

LAND REMEDIATION RELIEF

Commercial property owners, developers, and investors are eligible for land remediation relief. This is a tax relief system that allows for claims on any expenses associated with the decontamination of commercial premises. This includes the removal of asbestos and other harmful contaminants.

CHAPTER 28
CONCLUSION

I very much hope that you've enjoyed reading this book. It's been a pleasure to write and has reminded me of just how many commercial deals I've done over the years. As I said in the introduction, whether you are new to investing in commercial property or already investing and want to do more, I hope this book has given you the necessary insight and knowledge to successfully navigate the world of commercial property, which is what I set out to do.

My primary aim has been to demonstrate how I have dealt with the many situations and challenges that have arisen during my career in commercial property; and that it's best to be proactive and make deals happen, rather than sit back and wait for others to do it for you. I hope I've given you confidence in your dealings with other landlords, as well as tenants, and commercial agents, not to mention with your solicitors.

For the readers with years of experience, I hope this book has also reminded you, as it did me, to sharpen up your act over certain things; as well as there being points raised that will be useful in your property dealings going forward.

I truly believe there are exceptional opportunities currently within the commercial property sector to make great gains, whether you are looking to retain the property for long-term investment or to obtain a change of use and sell the investment on.

When you can buy a property that, in some instances, would cost five times more to now, surely there must be some profit in there somewhere. I believe we are in exceptional times and that we are unlikely to see again for many, many years, and we need to take full advantage of that situation as best as we can.

It only really leaves me to thank you very much for reading my book. If you have enjoyed it, then please tell other people and, if possible, leave a review. I do hope that at some point in the future we meet, either when I'm speaking at an event or at one of my seminars. The only time I probably don't want to meet you is in a vacant commercial property that I am interested in buying!

May I wish you all the very best and all the luck in the world of investing and trading in commercial property. And as they say, "The harder I work, the luckier I become."